IBM® SmartCloud® Essentials

Navigate and Use the IBM® SmartCloud® portfolio
for building cloud solutions

Edwin Schouten

PUBLISHING

BIRMINGHAM - MUMBAI

IBM® SmartCloud® Essentials

First published: December 2013

Production Reference: 1131213

Published by Packt Publishing Ltd.
Livery Place
35 Livery Street
Birmingham B3 2PB, UK.

ISBN 978-1-78217-064-8

www.packtpub.com

Cover Image by Erol Staveley (erols@packtpub.com)

Credits

Author
Edwin Schouten

Reviewer
Luis A. Guirigay

Acquisition Editor
Vinay Argekar

Commissioning Editor
Neil Alexander
Subho Gupta

Technical Editors
Aparna Chand
Amit Singh

Project Coordinator
Suraj Bist

Proofreader
Lucy Rowland

Indexer
Meriammal Chettiyar

Graphics
Ronak Dhruv

Production Coordinator
Melwyn D'sa

Cover Work
Melwyn D'sa

About the Author

Edwin Schouten is a Master IT Architect for IBM Global Technology Services. He is a Council Member and the Domain Champion for Cloud Computing in the IBM Benelux Technical Experts Council (TEC).

He has 15 years of experience in IT, holds a Master of Science in IT Architecture, is the Open Group Master Certified IT Architect, IBM Expert Level IT Architect, and IBM Certified Solution Advisor for Cloud Computing Architecture V3.

He is also a frequent speaker/panelist at cloud computing events, active member of Dutch cloud standardization bodies Platform Outsourcing Nederland and NEN, and blogger on his own website, edwinschouten.nl, with featured posts on Wired Insights, The Atlantic, Thoughts on Cloud, and Computable.nl.

You can reach Edwin at packt@edwinschouten.nl and his Twitter handle is @schoutene.

First and foremost I want to thank Martin van der Meer for his guidance and support during the writing of this book and my career development in general. I also want to specifically mention Rahul Jain for his reviewing efforts of this book. Other IBM® SmartCloud® team members to acknowledge are Dominique Vernier, Kit Linton, Frederic Mottiat, Alex Amies, Andrew Jones, Alfred Schilder, and Tiffany Townsend, and not to forget the authors of the developerWorks® articles that are referenced in this book.

Last but not least, I want to thank my wife Esther for her support throughout my many endeavors, and my wonderful children Daan and Sofie for the joy they bring to my life. I also want to thank my parents, Paul and Tine; sister, Cynthia; other close relatives; and friends who have supported me.

About the Reviewer

Luis A. Guirigay is an IT Architect at IBM with over 15 years experience in deployment, administration, support, analysis, design, and development of business applications focusing on delivering excellence with industry leading IBM platforms. His areas of expertise include deployment, infrastructure, high availability, disaster recovery, development, system tuning, troubleshooting, and everything else related to IBM Social and Collaboration solutions.

He is an IBM Certified Administrator for virtually all versions of IBM Connections, WebSphere Portal, Domino, Sametime, and Quickr as well as an IBM Certified Developer in Domino and an IBM Certified Instructor. Luis has published multiple developerWorks articles and IBM Redbooks related to Domino, Workplace, DB2, and System i. His speaking engagements include multiple User Group Conferences in North America as well in IBM Connect (also known as Lotusphere) and IBM workshops in the United States and LATAM. You can follow Luis at @lguiriga or e-mail him at lguiriga@us.ibm.com.

He has also worked on a few other books before, such as *Implementing IBM Lotus Domino 7 for i5/OS* (http://www.redbooks.ibm.com/abstracts/sg247311.html), *Preparing for and Tuning the SQL Query Engine on DB2 for i5/OS* (http://www.redbooks.ibm.com/abstracts/sg246598.html?Open), *Deploying IBM Workplace Collaboration Services on the IBM System i5 Platform* (http://www.redbooks.ibm.com/abstracts/sg246640.html?Open), and *IBM Lotus Sametime 8 Essentials: A User's Guide* (http://www.packtpub.com/ibm-lotus-sametime-8-essentials-a-users-guide/book).

> Even though being a reviewer for a book doesn't take nearly as much time as writing it, it still takes some time away from your family. So thanks to them for allowing me to take this time, which enabled me to be a part of this great book.

www.PacktPub.com

Support files, eBooks, discount offers, and more

You might want to visit www.PacktPub.com for support files and downloads related to your book.

Did you know that Packt offers eBook versions of every book published, with PDF and ePub files available? You can upgrade to the eBook version at www.PacktPub.com and as a print book customer, you are entitled to a discount on the eBook copy. Get in touch with us at service@packtpub.com for more details.

At www.PacktPub.com, you can also read a collection of free technical articles, sign up for a range of free newsletters and receive exclusive discounts and offers on Packt books and eBooks.

http://PacktLib.PacktPub.com

Do you need instant solutions to your IT questions? PacktLib is Packt's online digital book library. Here, you can access, read and search across Packt's entire library of books.

Why Subscribe?

- Fully searchable across every book published by Packt
- Copy and paste, print and bookmark content
- On demand and accessible via web browser

Free Access for Packt account holders

If you have an account with Packt at www.PacktPub.com, you can use this to access PacktLib today and view nine entirely free books. Simply use your login credentials for immediate access.

Instant Updates on New Packt Books

Get notified! Find out when new books are published by following @PacktEnterprise on Twitter, or the *Packt Enterprise* Facebook page.

Table of Contents

Preface

IBM® SmartCloud® Essentials takes you through the basics of cloud computing and covers the wide range of cloud components, services, and solutions in the IBM® SmartCloud® portfolio. This portfolio offers cloud solutions ranging from public to private cloud and infrastructure-as-a-service (IaaS) to business-process-as-a-service (BPaaS) solutions.

To make the concepts used in cloud computing more tangible, we zoom in to do a gradual deep-dive into one of IBM's public infrastructure-as-a-service (IaaS) cloud solutions; IBM® SmartCloud® Enterprise. Throughout the book you will gradually build an understanding of the concepts and practical uses of IBM® SmartCloud® Enterprise, entwined with building some hands-on experience along the way.

In the last chapter of the book, *Chapter 6, Further Developments*, we zoom out again to take a bird's eye view on what the future of cloud computing offered by IBM may be.

What this book covers

Chapter 1, IBM® SmartCloud®, covers the essentials of cloud computing and discovers what IBM has to offer in the cloud computing arena, guided by the IBM® SmartCloud® portfolio.

Chapter 2, IBM® SmartCloud® Enterprise, makes it more pragmatic by introducing the similarly named IBM public cloud solution. In this chapter we introduce the cloud service, discover the resource model, and provide an overview of its basic and premium services.

Chapter 3, Getting Started, focuses on the popular uses of IBM® SmartCloud® Enterprise and, exemplary for infrastructure cloud solutions in general, builds some hands-on experience by working with the SCE management console to get services provisioned.

Chapter 4, Advanced Use-cases, looks at advanced functions of IBM® SmartCloud® Enterprise such as using the REST (and other) API, image management, securing resources, back up and restore, monitoring instances, and high availability.

Chapter 5, There's an Ecosystem for That, elaborates the off-the-shelf solutions in the public image catalog containing both IBM and IBM Business Partners software products.

Chapter 6, Further Developments, zooms out again to the level of abstraction we started with in *Chapter 1, IBM® SmartCloud®*, only to take a little peak into the future by discussing platform services on top of IBM® SmartCloud® Enterprise, acquisitions, and other valuable sources of information.

Appendix, A Brief History, provides the full history of IBM® SmartCloud® Enterprise in chronological order.

What you need for this book

This book assumes that you have installed Eclipse™, only for using the *deployment utility tool* as described in *Chapter 4, Advanced Use-cases*. It can be downloaded from the website www.eclipse.org.

Who this book is for

This book is for **anyone** who wants to get a grasp of what cloud computing is and what IBM is doing in the area of cloud computing. For this group the book covers the practical side of cloud computing in *Chapter 1, IBM® SmartCloud®*, and offers a peek into the near future in *Chapter 6, Further Developments*.

Second, the book is also intended for readers with a technical background, such as IT specialists and IT architects. For this group, *Chapter 2* to *Chapter 5* takes the reader through the cloud computing resource model, using IBM® SmartCloud® Enterprise as an example, and gradually builds understanding of and experience with IBM® SmartCloud® Enterprise.

Conventions

In this book, you will find a number of styles of text that distinguish between different kinds of information. Here are some examples of these styles, and an explanation of their meaning.

Code words in text are shown as follows: "We can include other contexts through the use of the include directive."

Any command-line input or output is written as follows:

```
...
<Image>
    <ImageID>20025207</ImageID>
        <Name>Red Hat Enterprise Linux 6.3</Name>
...
```

New terms and **important words** are shown in bold. Words that you see on the screen, in menus or dialog boxes for example, appear in the text like this: "The SCE management console, specifically on the **Support** page, where many resources are directly available or just one click away in the **Documentation Library**, **Video Library**, and **Asset Catalog**."

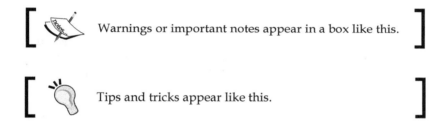

[Warnings or important notes appear in a box like this.]

[Tips and tricks appear like this.]

Reader feedback

Feedback from our readers is always welcome. Let us know what you think about this book—what you liked or may have disliked. Reader feedback is important for us to develop titles that you really get the most out of.

To send us general feedback, simply send an e-mail to feedback@packtpub.com, and mention the book title via the subject of your message.

If there is a topic that you have expertise in and you are interested in either writing or contributing to a book, see our author guide on www.packtpub.com/authors.

Customer support

Now that you are the proud owner of a Packt book, we have a number of things to help you to get the most from your purchase.

Errata

Although we have taken every care to ensure the accuracy of our content, mistakes do happen. If you find a mistake in one of our books—maybe a mistake in the text or the code—we would be grateful if you would report this to us. By doing so, you can save other readers from frustration and help us improve subsequent versions of this book. If you find any errata, please report them by visiting www.packtpub.com/submit-errata, selecting your book, clicking on the **errata submission form** link, and entering the details of your errata. Once your errata are verified, your submission will be accepted and the errata will be uploaded on our website, or added to any list of existing errata, under the Errata section of that title. Any existing errata can be viewed by selecting your title from www.packtpub.com/support.

Piracy

Piracy of copyright material on the Internet is an ongoing problem across all media. At Packt, we take the protection of our copyright and licenses very seriously. If you come across any illegal copies of our works, in any form, on the Internet, please provide us with the location address or website name immediately so that we can pursue a remedy.

Please contact us at copyright@packtpub.com with a link to the suspected pirated material.

We appreciate your help in protecting our authors, and our ability to bring you valuable content.

Questions

You can contact us at questions@packtpub.com if you are having a problem with any aspect of the book, and we will do our best to address it.

1
IBM® SmartCloud®

In this first chapter we will cover the essentials of cloud computing and set the stage for the chapters to follow. We will briefly cover the essential characteristics, business benefits, and organizational impact of cloud computing to avoid any misconception later on in the book.

After this we discover what IBM® has to offer in the cloud computing arena in the IBM® SmartCloud® portfolio. From this portfolio, we find out which foundational components, cloud services, and cloud solutions IBM has available.

Lastly, we cover the strengths and weaknesses of IBM® SmartCloud® Enterprise within the portfolio before we learn how to get started with this specific cloud solution in the next chapter.

A brief history of IBM

Before we start with cloud computing and the IBM® SmartCloud® portfolio, let's first briefly look at the history of IBM. International Business Machines Corporation (or IBM) is a leading technology and service company which has been delivering innovative technology solutions for over 100 years. IBM serves clients in over 170 countries, has over 4,00,000 employees worldwide, is the third most valuable brand worldwide, and has delivered the most U.S. patents for 20 years in a row. To quote Ginni Rometty, Chief Executive Officer, IBM:

> "IBM is an innovation company. We pursue continuous transformation both in what we do and how we do it – always remixing to higher value in our offerings and skills, in our operations and management practices, and in the transformational capabilities we deliver to our clients."

Over that last few years, IBM has been heavily engaged on the Smarter Planet® strategy, which recognizes that, each and every day, the world is getting more:

- **Instrumented**: Computers in any shape and size are nowadays everywhere. Think of smartphones, home automation, electric cars, and alternative power sources such as windmills and solar panels.

- **Interconnected**: Exchanging data to work together. Think of an on-demand streaming video on your television set, using your smartphone to control your lights or central heating, but also cities being able to control traffic better using data from surveillance cameras and sensors in the road.

- **Intelligent**: Using the data gathered (interconnected) from the many sensors (instruments) around us to get information and even new insights that enable us all to do things smarter.

In 2011 IBM announced the Smarter Computing IT framework, as part of the Smarter Planet strategy, which is based on three key principles: designing systems for data, optimizing systems for specific workloads, and managing systems in using a cloud computing architecture. As the title suggests, this book will only cover the cloud computing part of the Smarter Computing IT framework.

All IBM cloud computing solutions are bundled in the IBM® SmartCloud® portfolio which will be elaborated further on in this chapter. From the next chapter onwards, we will focus specifically on the IBM® SmartCloud® Enterprise in particular, as this public cloud service allows us to example many of the characteristics that are essential to cloud computing.

Beware of fake clouds!

Before going into detail about the IBM® SmartCloud® portfolio, we will touch upon the main characteristics of cloud computing. Although you would think that by now, since the term cloud computing dates back from 2008, we would all know characteristics an IT solutions should have to be considered cloud computing.

Unfortunately this is not the case, but this is not unique to cloud computing alone. Think of service oriented architecture (SOA) for instance, which was never really understood by the public at large.

Thankfully, standards for cloud computing are emerging, which most of the larger IT providers are adopting. So, get educated! Not with IT provided – marketing infused – collateral, but by using knowledge of well-renowned standardization bodies.

Good examples of standards and standardization bodies are the National Institute of Standards and Technology (NIST) at www.nist.gov/itl/cloud, the Open Group® at www.opengroup.org/subjectareas/cloudcomputing, Cloud Standards Customer Council (CSCC) at www.cloud-council.org, Cloud Computing Use Case Discussion Group at cloudusecases.org, OpenStack® at www.openstack.org, and OASIS® TOSCA at www.oasis-open.org/committees/tosca.

The definition

To get a common understanding on cloud computing, which you will need for the following chapters, let's start with the basics: the essential characteristics and service and deployment models. For this, we will use one of the standardization bodies described earlier, NIST to be more specific, as the NIST definition has become the de facto definition of cloud computing:

> *"Cloud computing is a model for enabling ubiquitous, convenient, on-demand network access to a shared pool of configurable computing resources (e.g., networks, servers, storage, applications, and services) that can be rapidly provisioned and released with minimal management effort or service provider interaction."*

 Read about the NIST definition of cloud computing at csrc.nist.gov/publications/nistpubs/800-145/SP800-145.pdf.

Although this widely-adopted description of what makes a cloud computing solution is very valuable, it is not very tangible or easy to understand. So let's dive a little deeper into cloud computing and why it's different than just visualization alone, which is commonly mistaken to be cloud computing as well.

The following image shows that cloud computing is composed of five essential characteristics, three deployment models, and four service models as shown in the following figure:

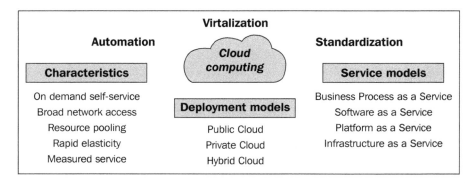

Let's look a bit closer at each of the characteristics, service models, and deployment models in the next sections.

Five essential characteristics

The essential characteristics can be elaborated as follows:

- **On-demand self-service**: Users are able to provision cloud computing resources without requiring human interaction, mostly done though a web-based self-service portal (management console).

- **Broad network access**: Cloud computing resources are accessible over the network, supporting heterogeneous client platforms such as mobile devices and workstations.

- **Resource pooling**: Service multiple customers from the same physical resources, by securely separating the resources on logical level.

- **Rapid elasticity**: Resources are provisioned and released on-demand and/or automated based on triggers or parameters. This will make sure your application will have exactly the capacity it needs at any point of time.

- **Measured service**: Resource usage are monitored, measured, and reported (billed) transparently based on utilization. In short, pay for use.

As we see, cloud computing is much more than just virtualization. It's really about utilizing technology "as a service". Users need little to no knowledge on the details of how a particular service is implemented, on which hardware, on how many CPU's, and so on. All that's important for a user is to have good understanding of what the service offers—and what it does not—and how to operate the self-service portal.

Four service models

According to NIST there are three service models: infrastructure (**IaaS**), platform (**PaaS**), and software as-a-service (**SaaS**). To get a better understanding on what each of the service models comprises, refer to the following image that depicts the layers of which atypical IT solution consists:

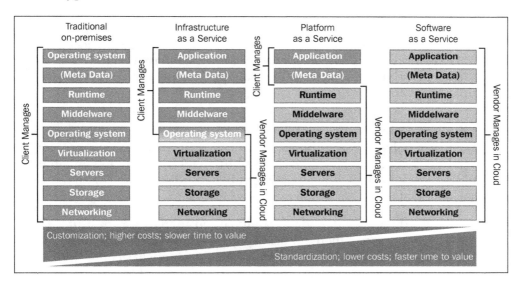

An infrastructure as a service solution should include vendor-managed network, storage, servers, and virtualization layers for a client to run their application and data on. Next, platform as a service build on top of infrastructure as a service adding vendor-managed middleware such as web, application, and database software. Software as a service again builds on top of that, most of the time adding applications that implement specific user functionality such as email, CRM, or HRM.

Interestingly enough, IBM and other major IT and analyst firms have added a fourth service model, namely business process as a service (**BPaaS**). Business process as a service, as the word implies, offers an entire horizontal or vertical business process and builds on top of any of the previously depicted cloud service models. See more tangible examples of business process as a service in the *IBM® SmartCloud® Solutions* section in this chapter.

Three deployment models

Now we know what cloud computing is and in which services we can consume it. Let's wrap up the basics with how cloud providers in turn can deploy cloud computing solutions to business and consumers.

Three main deployment models can be considered: private, public, and hybrid. Although this sounds pretty easy, these deployment models should be considered more as a spectrum of delivery options than a limited set of options:

- **Private**: A single-tenant cloud solution utilizing hardware and software owned by the client, physically located inside the client firewall or even data center. Most of the time upfront investment is required, similar to traditional IT.

- **Public**: A multi-tenant cloud solution delivered from shared hardware and software owned by the cloud service provider, physically located outside the clients' private network (mostly the Internet) and data centers. Most of the time these services are truly pay for use and do not require upfront investment.

- **Hybrid**: An IT landscape comprised of both private and public cloud solutions. Hybrid is expected to be the most adopted deployment model because it delivers best of breed solutions for all needs. A client can, for example, implement a private cloud solution for applications containing highly sensitive data while utilizing public cloud solutions for all non-sensitive data.

As mentioned, the deployment models should be considered as a spectrum. Think of who owns the hardware, where the service is physically delivered from, who manages each of the IT layers of the service model, how network connectivity is arranged, how the payment model is constructed, and more of these variables.

 To learn more on what cloud computing is and how to take advantage, download the e-book, *Cloud Services for Dummies*, free of charge at http://ow.ly/kYahH.

The value of cloud services

Now that we have covered what cloud computing, is let's briefly cover what the value of utilizing cloud services can be. We specifically mention "can be", as the true value can be different per application. There's no one-size-fits-all cloud solution available, as many different applications exist in the world and many organizations utilize applications differently.

However as a general rule, one of the benefits of cloud computing is increased efficiency; services are rapidly deployed and ready for use in a matter of minutes versus the weeks or months it traditionally takes. But, there is more to cloud computing than just getting your computed resources, storage capacity, or application as a service within minutes. Some examples are:

- **Business agility**: Getting the compute resources you need when you need them. This will drastically shorten the time for new projects to get started, resulting in a quicker and ultimately more predictive time-to-market. Being able to deliver results faster, cheaper, and with more quality might just give a business the competitive edge it needs.

- **New business models**: Using or combining readily available cloud services into a service allows us to define new and innovative business models with ease. This can result in new value propositions and revenue streams.

- **Less operational issues**: Reduce issues and defects significantly by utilizing standardized services. This will increase business continuity and reduce time spent on operational issues. Secondly, cloud computing can also allow us to deploy the same service or topology of services repetitively, with the same predictable result every time.

- **Less capital expense**: There is some debate about the value of shifting from a capital expense (CapEx) model to an operational expense (OpEx) model. The overall feeling is that, specifically for short and midterm projects, the OpEx model is more attractive because there are no long term financial commitments.

As we see, there can be quite some value in using cloud services. But, let us remember that the exact value we perceive and achieve will be different for each application and the application's entire life cycle.

The IBM® SmartCloud® portfolio

Now that we have covered the inevitable basics of cloud computing, let's see what IBM has to offer in the cloud arena. It will come as no surprise that IBM, as a hardware and software vendor, and business and technology services provider, has a lot to offer. IBM in fact has a unique position in the industry— by bringing together key cloud technologies, deep process knowledge, and a network of global delivery centers— and a broad portfolio of cloud software and solutions.

All IBM cloud computing services are bundled in the IBM® SmartCloud® portfolio, which consists of three unique segments as the following IBM image depicts.

Each of the segments — IBM® SmartCloud® Foundation, IBM® SmartCloud® Services and IBM® SmartCloud® Solutions — has a specific set of cloud services and can be loosely mapped to the cloud service and deployment models.

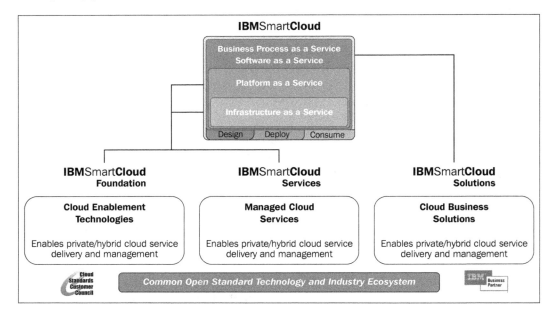

Overlaying all segments are the consulting, implementation, migration, and management services to assist clients in defining their business cloud strategy, either becoming a cloud service provider or adopting cloud services, and start utilizing cloud services.

An important asset for these services is the **Cloud Computing Reference Architecture (CCRA)**, a blueprint or guide for architecting cloud computing implementations. The CCRA, based on years of experience of working with customers who have implemented cloud computing solutions, has captured best practices and patterns for many different cloud computing usage scenarios.

The most recent version of the CCRA, at time of writing Version 3, focuses specifically on four main cloud adoption patterns:

- **Cloud-enabled data center**: How an organization can build a private IaaS solution and hybrid cloud integration
- **Platform Services**: Extending the cloud-enable data center pattern with PaaS solutions
- **Building SaaS**: Build value propositions and use cases for SaaS solutions
- **Cloud Service Provider**: How organizations can build a "commercial" cloud to become a cloud service provider themselves

An interesting aspect of the CCRA is that everyone is free to learn about it and can prove that they have mastered it by certifying as IBM Certified Solution Advisor—Cloud Computing Architecture V3.

 Find more on the IBM CCRA at http://ow.ly/kYprq and CCRA certification at www-03.ibm.com/certify/certs/50001103.shtml.

Another thing to note is IBM's commitment to open cloud standards. IBM has a long history of supporting standards and open source initiatives. IBM, for instance, joined the OpenStack Foundation as Platinum-level sponsor in 2012 to leverage extensive client experience and the services in the IBM® SmartCloud® portfolio. Adoption of open cloud standards will ultimately prevent cloud consumers having issues with vendor lock-in which allows cloud consumers to utilize the growing market of cloud services without hesitation.

 See more on open cloud standards IBM supports in *Chapter 6, Further Developments.*

IBM® SmartCloud® Foundation

The first segment of the IBM® SmartCloud® portfolio is IBM® SmartCloud® Foundation. IBM® SmartCloud® Foundation refers to a set of hardware and software components available for enterprises or service providers to build their own private or hybrid cloud solutions. IBM® SmartCloud® Foundation delivers a unique set of capabilities to implement integrated cloud service delivery and management. Some examples are, but are not limited to:

- Hardware and software enabling technologies to allow the customer to build their own private cloud part-by-part, deploy workloads across multiple cloud deployment models, and integrate applications in the cloud with little effort. Examples of software products are:
  - ° Provisioning and life cycle management software products such as IBM® SmartCloud® Entry, IBM® SmartCloud® Provisioning, and IBM® SmartCloud® Orchestration
  - ° Monitoring and performance software like IBM® SmartCloud® Monitoring
  - ° WebSphere® Cast Iron® Cloud integration software and appliances
- PureSystems™ expert integrated systems capture and automate what experts do — from the infrastructure to the application — to make IT easy to deploy and manage. PureSystems delivers integrated and tuned hardware and software resources in ready-to-go, workload-optimized systems.
- IBM Cloud Service Provider Platform gives **Communication Service Providers** (**CSP**) the ability to rapidlyand cost-effectively create, manage, and deliver high quality services using an advanced, scalable, carrier-grade integrated service management platform designed for CSPs.

IBM® SmartCloud® Services

The second segment of the IBM® SmartCloud® portfolio is IBM® SmartCloud® Services. IBM® SmartCloud® Services refer to a set of "public" IT cloud services delivered to enterprises. These IT services are covering the infrastructure and platform as a service space. They are specifically targeting large enterprise needs, providing enhanced service level agreement, security, and reliability required to serve production workloads.

As we have learned previously, a one-size-fits-all solution does not exist. IBM, therefore, differentiates two different types of cloud service, aligned to two different types of workloads: cloud-enabled workloads (system of record) and cloud-centric workloads (system of engagement).

Each workload has different characteristics, requiring a different infrastructure to support it:

- Systems of record are passive, storing data and provide access/processing capabilities to interact with it
- Systems of engagement encompass data and processing capabilities that include active stimulus/response functions

The following image from IBM shows the two types of workloads and depicts some of the unique characteristics:

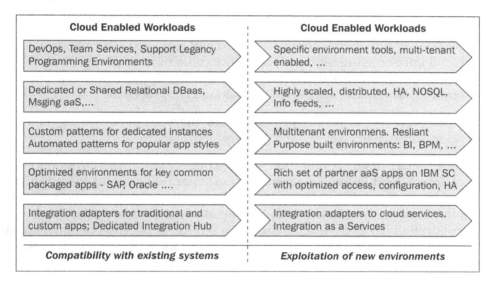

 More on the difference between systems of record versus systems of engagement can be found in the Forbes blog post at www.forbes. com/sites/joshbersin/2012/08/16/the-move-from- systems-of-record-to-systems-of-engagement.

Continuing with the IBM® SmartCloud® Services, let's look at the infrastructure services offered. The infrastructure as a service offerings consist of:

- IBM® SmartCloud® Enterprise, designed and built for cloud-centric workloads, enables enterprise clients to expand on internal development and test efforts, or accelerates new development and test projects via the cloud, with instant access to computing and storage resources, and IBM middleware and application life cycle management capabilities through IBM's secure, scalable cloud delivery model. In July 2013, IBM further strengthened its cloud-centric capabilities by acquiring SoftLayer Technologies, refer to *Chapter 6, Further Developments*, for more details.

- IBM® SmartCloud® Enterprise+ is purposefully built for cloud-enabled workloads and offers a complete hosted and managed self-configurable cloud infrastructure service. This service contains multiple levels of isolation and 99.9 percent availability, ideal for migration of mission critical and strategic workloads, supported with cloud ITIL processes.

On top of the preceding infrastructure as services offerings, the following platforms as a service are available:

- IBM® SmartCloud® Application Services offers platform services on top of SmartCloud Enterprise to provide customers with an end-to-end suite of tools for application development, deployment, and integration. It will offer integrated, team-based development environments on the cloud, application resources like database as a service, application deployment and management with purpose built services, and integration to synchronize data and processes across applications.

- IBM® SmartCloud® for SAP Applications is a private shared cloud solution for business critical SAP system landscapes with production and non-production SAP systems. Certified SAP specialist for all relevant SAP products and technologies support the SAP systems in a 24 x 7 mode and ensure the highest service quality which are also defined in service level agreements.

- IBM® SmartCloud® for Oracle applications is also a private shared cloud solution, but for business critical Oracle applications. It offers Oracle-managed services in a platform as a service (PaaS) mode for the full range of Oracle products on all VM options of the IBM® SmartCloud® Enterprise+ offering. As you might expect from a cloud service, it offers a flexible pricing model and payment options and significant improvement in time to service as compared to traditional deployments.

 More on these PaaS solutions will be covered in more detail in *Chapter 6, Further Developments*.

Finally, the IBM® SmartCloud® Resilience suite offers a flexible, automated backup and recovery-managed service for all critical data, located onsite or offsite, using public and/or private cloud technology.

IBM® SmartCloud® Solutions

Last but not least, IBM® SmartCloud® Solutions refer to software and business processes delivered by IBM as a service. The solutions are grouped into specific verticals: business analytics and optimization solutions, social business solutions, smarter commerce solutions, and smarter cities. Example services are, but not limited to the following:

- Business analytics and optimization solutions such as IBM Cognos®, IBM SPSS®, and IBM BAO Strategic IP Insight platform
- Social business solutions such as IBM® SmartCloud® for Social Business, which has over 18 million users worldwide collaborating in the cloud, within and across company firewalls
- Smarter Commerce™ solutions such as the suits of IBM DemandTec®, IBM Coremetrics®, IBM Emptoris®, and IBM Unica® offer great functionality right from the cloud for buying, selling, marketing, and servicing
- Smarter Cities® solutions such as IBM Intelligent Operations Center provide leaders the tools to analyze data for better decisions, anticipate problems to resolve them proactively, coordinate resources to operate effectively, drive sustainable economic growth, and prosperity for their citizens

BPaaS offerings are also part of the IBM® SmartCloud® Solutions segment, offering for instance, service desk, payment, and expense reporting solutions.

Summary

In this chapter we have learned a bit about the history of IBM, and that cloud computing is solidly embedded in the company's strategy. Next we covered the basics: what cloud computing is (and isn't), and what its business values can be, before covering the highlights of the IBM® SmartCloud® portfolio and complete set of cloud services readily available for clients to use.

In the next chapters, we will zoom-in on one of the previously mentioned cloud services, IBM® SmartCloud® Enterprise. This cloud solution is a very good example for us to learn how an IaaS solution can be operated, utilized, and what use-cases it can support.

IBM® SmartCloud® Enterprise

As we have seen in the previous chapter, IBM® has a wide variety of cloud computing solutions in the market. From this chapter on, this book will cover IBM® SmartCloud® Enterprise, one of IBM's public IaaS solutions. The information in the following chapters is based on the current version of IBM® SmartCloud® Enterprise (at time of writing this book, it is version 2.3).

Although a lot of information is available about IBM® SmartCloud® Enterprise's capabilities, it's not always easy to find. This book will provide you with an overview of those capabilities, and how to use and configure IBM® SmartCloud® Enterprise to fit your business needs.

In this chapter, we will start to understand the basic concepts and learn about the basic and premium services available. We will learn how to work with the basic functions by navigating to the self-service portal called SCE management console and how to quickly get a cost estimate for any specific configuration. Lastly, we will cover how to order the basic and premium services online and where to find support.

Introduction

In the previous chapter, we have already touched upon IBM® SmartCloud® Enterprise briefly as one of the two (publicly) managed IaaS solutions available.

To recap, IBM® SmartCloud® Enterprise is a flexible computing IaaS solution designed to provide clients with rapid access to enterprise class cloud environments. The service provides us with a SCE management console, extensive image catalog containing IBM and non-IBM software products, and the ability to upload our own images, while allowing the user full control over all the resources provisioned above the managed hypervisor.

IBM® SmartCloud® Enterprise has been available since May 2010, matching the needs of the market at that time by primarily focusing on test and development workloads. One year later, in May 2011, the service offered full support to production workloads as well.

To improve the support for production workloads, IBM® SmartCloud® Enterprise officially achieved certification of the ISO/IEC 27001:2005 standard in June 2012. This security standard provides a framework to ensure that the certified organization addresses the required security needs of its customers.

This is just a brief summary. Find the full history of IBM® SmartCloud® Enterprise in chronological order in *Appendix, A Brief History*.

Understanding the basic concepts

The basic concepts of IBM® SmartCloud® Enterprise are based on a couple of main resources: virtual machine instances, block storage volumes, software bundles, and images. Before we describe these resources in more detail, let's draw the bigger picture of these resources and their relationships:

- We start with a client that wants to use resources from the cloud, located in an IBM® SmartCloud® Enterprise data center at a location of their choice. The client is connected to this location either via a VPN connection and the Internet, or with both.
- Every location has a set of software bundles, an image catalog containing at least public images, and may contain virtual machine instances and block storage volumes.
- Every virtual machine instance is created and provisioned from an image in the image catalog, potentially including one or more software bundles.
- Every virtual machine instance has attributes such as capacity type and IP address. Optional attributes can be VLAN when a private network is needed, and SSH key to securely connect to Linux virtual machine instances.

The following figure shows the resources we just covered, including the ways to connect to the locations and the resources available in each location:

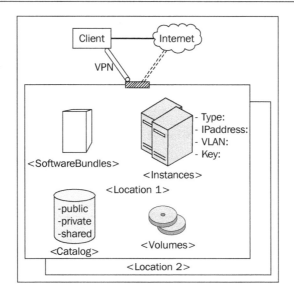

In the next chapter, we will revisit these resources and look more in depth at their relationships and attributes. Some of the resources covered are considered to be basic services such as the virtual machine instances and Internet connectivity, as these form the basis of most cloud configurations. Others are optional premium services. In the next sections, we will look at how we can utilize the resources, first the basic services followed by the premium services.

Basic services

This section covers the basic services, which are fundamental to the cloud solution. We will cover the most essential information. A full description of all the basic and premium services can be found in the service description webpage at `www-935.ibm.com/services/us/en/cloud-enterprise/contracts/services_description.html`.

Before we start elaborating the basic services one by one in the following sections, let's look at what a standard cloud server consists of. A standard server configuration will normally consist of a virtual machine instance, virtual local storage, and a network access method to connect to it. Let's look at each of these components, along with the images in the images catalog and support options.

Virtual machine instances

A virtual machine instance consists of one or more virtual CPUs, virtual memory, and virtual local storage. In IBM® SmartCloud® Enterprise, we have a choice of 10 virtual machine instance sizes and 10 different CPU-RAM combinations (32- or 64-bit) to pick from as the following tables depict:

Virtual machine instances (32-bit)	Copper	Bronze	Silver	Gold
Virtual CPUs (1.25GHz)	1	1	2	4
Virtual memory (GB)	2	2	4	4
Virtual local storage (GB)	60	235	410	410

Virtual machine instances (64-bit)	Copper	Bronze	Silver	Gold	Platinum	Platinum M2
Virtual CPUs (1.25GHz)	2	2	4	8	16	16
Virtual memory (GB)	4	4	8	16	16	32
Virtual local storage (GB)	60	910	1084	1084	2108	2108

For the most updated version of this table, please visit `www-935.ibm.com/services/us/en/cloud-enterprise/tab-details-server-configurations.html`.

Virtual machine instances can be provisioned as standalone servers, but also in combination with other instances to build more sophisticated configurations. This allows us to support, for example, a layered web server architecture. In *Chapter 4, Advanced Use-cases* we will cover some of the options for building and running more sophisticated configurations.

The usage charges for a virtual machine instance include charges for virtual compute resources and charges for the operating system license. Usage charges will depend on whether we select to use a reserved capacity, where we pay an upfront fee for guaranteed available capacity at a discounted cost, or select unreserved capacity basis. This can be selected during the ordering process.

See the charges schedule for more details or use the IBM® SmartCloud® Enterprise Monthly Cost Estimator to automatically calculate the best capacity plan for any specific configuration. The charges schedule is available at `www-935.ibm.com/services/us/en/cloud-enterprise/contracts/charges_schedule.html`.

The IBM® SmartCloud® Enterprise Monthly Cost Estimator will be covered in more detail later on in this chapter.

Virtual local storage

The virtual local storage, also called instance or ephemeral storage, will get deleted with the deletion of the virtual machine instance it comes with. In the section on premium services, we will describe how we can attach different types of storage to safeguard the virtual machine instance files independently.

Each of the 10 virtual machine instance sizes also has a default size of instance storage attached to it. During provisioning, we also have the option to provision a virtual machine's instance with a minimal amount of instance storage (60 GB), which will reduce provisioning times for large virtual machine instance types.

Network access methods

When configuring a virtual machine instance, the default option is that the server is accessible directly from the Internet. When directly connected to the Internet, the virtual machine instance gets a system-assigned IP address dynamically during its creation.

Premium services can be added such as setting up a secure connection to the cloud solution using the **Virtual Private Network (VPN)** technology, separating virtual machine instances using the private **Virtual Local Area Network (VLAN)** options, and using reserved IP addresses. These will be covered in the next section.

 Each virtual machine instance can have up to four IP addresses in total.

Image catalog

Every virtual machine instance is created from an image in the IBM® SmartCloud® Enterprise image catalog. The image catalog is logically separated into private, shared, and public catalogs which contain images only you can use, images that you have created but others can also use, and standard images that come with cloud solution respectively.

The public image catalog contains operating system images, different flavors of the Linux® and Microsoft Windows® operating systems, and images containing pre-installed applications along with the operating system. The latter offers a wide variety of applications with both IBM and non-IBM software products, further detailed in *Chapter 5, There's an Ecosystem for That*.

An up-to-date overview of all the images and license options can be found at www.ibm.com/developerworks/cloud/devtest.html.

The image catalog can also be appended with private images; there are also multiple ways to create our own images and solutions using IBM® SmartCloud® Enterprise. We will discuss some of these options in more detail in *Chapter 4, Advanced Use-cases*.

Support and maintenance

Naturally, we need some support facilities for additional guidance at times when unexpected things happen or issues occur. The default complementary support option is forum support. Also, any IT infrastructure needs maintenance. Now, let's look at how these are communicated.

Forum support

The IBM® SmartCloud® Enterprise forums are communities where you can share your ideas about the IBM® SmartCloud® Enterprise service and get help on your issues. The forum is available through the **Support** page of the SCE management console.

Additional support features such as 24 X 7 telephone support and direct access to the ticket system are also available as additional services, which will be described in the premium service section.

Maintenance windows

Scheduled maintenance windows are communicated through the header of the SCE management console by default. This header message is visible for every user and can be easily closed by clicking on the **Close** option in the upper-right corner. The downside to this way of communication, however, is that if your resources are running smooth and you don't visit the SCE management console too often, you might miss some of them.

To prevent this from happening, the maintenance messages can also be communicated via a mailing list, called the Enhanced Notification System. This mailing list is used automatically to notify you of the upcoming maintenance windows, unexpected outage information, and any pertinent information on the IBM® SmartCloud® Enterprise environment every time new information becomes available.

Subscribing to the mailing list is a two-step process:

1. Simply send an e-mail to `ibm_smartcloud_enterprise_notification-join@lists.ca.ibm.com`. The subject and body of the e-mail can be left blank. Any text entered there will get ignored by the system.

2. Once the e-mail is received, the system will send you a confirmation e-mail. Simply reply to that e-mail, leaving the subject line intact.

Once the confirmation is processed, you will be signed up for the list, and receive a standard welcome message.

Premium services

Now that we have discovered what the basic services are, let's see how these can be extended to allow more advanced configurations. There are three types of premium services available: network access, storage, and support options.

Storage options

It is quite obvious that the amount of storage provided with the virtual machine instance is not sufficient for our needs. We have the option to append the virtual machine instances with additional storage, which will remain until it is manually deleted, using block storage.

Block storage

Block storage, also called persistent storage, is ideal for applications with higher I/O requirements such as database files. Block storage is available in eight unit sizes: 60 GB, 256 GB, 512 GB, 1 TB, 2 TB, 4 TB, 8 TB, and 10 TB.

The usage charge is based on the number of gigabytes (GBs) ordered in each persistent storage block, independent of the actual used GBs, and the number of storage I/O access requests.

Interestingly, the images in the private image catalog are saved on block storage. In this case, we are only charged for the actual used GBs the private image consumes, independent of the I/O access requests.

Network options

As a premium service, virtual machine instances can also be connected to a secure connection using one or multiple VPN tunnels in an IBM® SmartCloud® Enterprise data center, connected to one or multiple VLANs in the data center, to separate instances from each other allowing secure multi-tier architectures.

[Servers with both a public Internet and private IP address can act as proxies to your backend servers, isolated on a VPN in the cloud.]

Virtual private network

Each VPN environment consists of up to five private VLANs, plus a VPN gateway with up to five tunnels for connecting to the data centers of your choice. Virtual machine instances that are provisioned with IP addresses on your private VLANs can only be accessed through the VPN gateway; they are not accessible from the Internet.

Virtual local area network

To use a VPN gateway in a cloud data center, you will need to provide an IP gateway on your side of the network to connect to the cloud data center.

Additionally, we can also use VLANs without a VPN connection, for instance to disallow direct connections to some of our servers for security reasons. A wide variety of options are described in the developerWorks® article *Build multiple VPNs and VLANs* at www.ibm.com/developerworks/cloud/library/cl-multiplevlans.

Reserved IP addresses

Along with the system-assigned IP addresses, we can also use reserved IP addresses for our virtual machine instances. The benefit of this is you always have the same IP address and DNS record to connect to it, even though you might have switched the underlying virtual server instance.

To request reserved IP addresses, simply use the SCE management console to submit an order for an IP address. By doing so, the system will allocate an IP address for us which is reserved for our exclusive use until we choose to delete the reservation. IP addresses are charged on a per-hour basis.

Additional support options

In cases where the complimentary forum support does not suit your requirements, you can extend this with either premium or advanced premium support services.

Premium support

The premium support option extends forum support by providing us with the following advantages:

- Round-the-clock telephone helpdesk routing office
- A web-based ticketing system to submit and review service requests
- Remote technical support to assist us in using the SCE management console, accessing services, creating instances, and managing image functions within the portal

This, however, does not include support for the operating systems and applications of the virtual machine instances. Such support may be available under a separate agreement from IBM (for example, software subscription and support agreement) or from a third-party vendor.

Advanced premium support

Advanced premium support builds on top of the premium support and adds severity-level-driven response times, from 30 minutes for severity 1 (severe business impact) to 24) hours for severity 4 (no business impact), and a **Service Level Agreement (SLA)** with refunds, should IBM not meet the committed response times.

Add-on operating system support

When we purchase a premium support service, we can choose to add support for the Linux or Microsoft Windows operating system that IBM provides with its images.

Estimating your cost

One of the characteristics of cloud computing is pay-for-use, which requires full transparency of the price of each of the elements multiplied by the times we used the elements. Now that we have covered all the basic and premium services, let's look at the charges associated with these services.

As mentioned previously, there is a charges schedule available online for this. But we can also use the Monthly Cost Estimator which allows us to quickly estimate the cost of any configuration that you build with IBM® SmartCloud® Enterprise. The first step of the 5-step process is shown in the following screenshot:

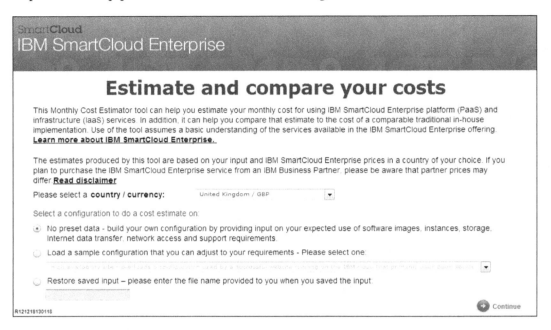

The Monthly Cost Estimator allows you to fill in the service configuration you need along with your estimate at the time of using the services. In the five steps, you will need to fill in the following details:

- The image(s) you will use to provision your instances from
- The virtual machine instance size(s) your image(s) require(s)
- Additional block or object storage, if any
- The network access method(s) and, if any network options needed
- Any additional support options, if needed

As you might have noticed, this process completely matches the build-up of this chapter. The final tab of the calculator allows you to compare the cost estimator outcome with a traditional IT solution.

The Monthly Cost Estimator can be found online at ww-935.ibm.com/services/us/igs/cloud-development/estimator/Tool.htm.

We can also save configurations we put into the calculator, and reload them when we need to alter the configuration at a different point in time.

Preparing to get started

Now that we understand the technical and financial details of IBM® SmartCloud® Enterprise, we can order access to the service online and/or order additional services to expand what we are already using.

Creating an account

If you have not done so already, IBM® SmartCloud® Enterprise can be easily ordered online at www.ibm.com/buycloud. The online order form is an easy 7-step process that takes us through all the basic and premium services you want to order, quite similar to the Monthly Cost Estimator:

1. Choose a plan to order. Select either **Unreserved virtual machine instances** or **Reserved capacity packages with preferred pricing**, as differentiated in the section **Virtual machine instance**, and click on **Continue**.

2. Select the premium services you need, such as **Object storage**, **VPN**, and **Additional support**, and click on **Continue**.

3. Then, you need to sign in with your IBM ID, which will be used as the user credentials to sign in to the IBM® SmartCloud® Enterprise management console once processed. If you don't have an IBM ID yet, you can create one here as well.

4. Fill in all the required fields to provide IBM the account details needed and click on **Continue**.

5. Read and accept the license agreement by selecting **I agree** and click on **Continue**.

6. Fill in your payment information such as the **Billing address** and **Purchase order information**, and click on **Continue**.

7. Confirm that all the information is correct and click on **Sign-up**.

Once the order form has been reviewed and submitted, your account will be activated within 5-10 business days, depending on your geography. Once activated, you will receive a welcome e-mail containing the IBM® SmartCloud® Enterprise welcome kit. The e-mail will be sent to the IBM ID e-mail address configured earlier.

Watch the video *How to purchase SmartCloud Enterprise, IBM's IaaS offering* to quickly learn how to order online at www.youtube.com/ watch?v=dPhr8rV8h6A.

Ordering premium services

If you already have an account, but would like to extend it with any of the premium services, the online additional services form can be used. This form can be found as one of the tabs available via the charges schedule URL that was previously provided.

 For some premium services such as VPN, an IBM representative will contact us to gather the technical information required to configure the service for us.

Navigating to the SCE management console

Once the account has been enabled, you can log on to the IBM® SmartCloud® Enterprise management console from where you have control over the basic services and most of the premium services that you have ordered. See the following screenshot which depicts the **Support** page of the SCE management console:

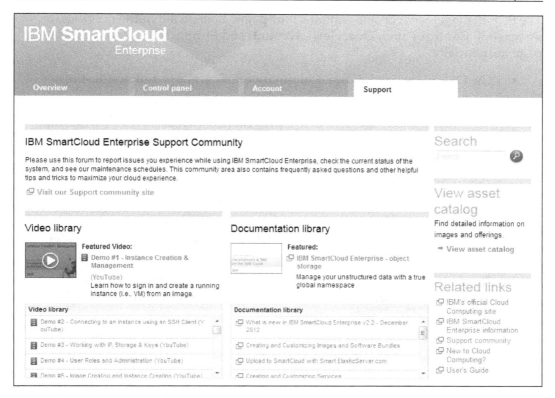

The SCE management console is the access point of the services, available via www. ibm.com/cloud/enterprise. From the management console, you are able to control all the basic services, get a list of your active instances, retrieve user statistics, find video demos and other useful resources.

 An alternative way to control your services is to use the IBM® SmartCloud® Enterprise API, which we will cover in details in the next chapter.

The SCE management console contains four pages as depicted in the previous screenshot: **Control panel**, **Overview**, **Account**, and **Support**. Let's look at each page individually:

- The **Overview** page shows a summary of our account and notifications.

- The **Control panel** page lets us do the following things:
    ○ View, manage, and delete provisioned virtual server instances and create new virtual server instances from the image catalog
    ○ View, manage, and delete the private images created from customized instances or imported images
    ○ View, add, manage, and delete persistent storage blocks
    ○ View, add, manage, and delete service instances offered as part of IBM® SmartCloud® Application Services, discussed in more detail in *Chapter 6, Further Developments*.

- The **Account** page holds your private keys, reserved IP addresses, an aggregation of your account and instance/image notifications, some global statistics, and basic user information.

- The **Support** page gives you access to the IBM Cloud communities and a diverse variety of other cloud materials. There, you will find the following information:
    ○ The Support Community Forum is the place to go for information on system status, answers to frequently asked questions, and tips on using the system.
    ○ Video Library contains demonstration videos on several topics such as how to create and manage images, setting up a VPN connection, and using firewalls.
    ○ Document Library contains documents to help you use the SCE management console. Among other things, it has a copy of the Welcome Kit and User Guide.
    ○ Asset Catalog contains additional documentation and many technical support files.

To get a feeling of using the SCE management console before you have access to it, the IBM® SmartCloud® simulator is available at `www-935.ibm.com/services/us/cloud/simulator/Main.swf`. In the next chapter, we will build some hands-on experience when we create our first virtual machine instance.

Summary

In this chapter, we have learned the basic IBM® SmartCloud® Enterprise resources model and the basic and premium services available. We have also covered where to find the most relevant documents, contracts, and all the prices right from the Internet. Finding out what your intended workload will cost beforehand is very valuable, so we have also covered how to use the Monthly Cost Estimator.

Lastly, we have covered how to navigate to the SCE management console and where to find the most basic functions. In the next chapters, we will cover more detailed functions and features of the services.

3
Getting Started

In this chapter, we get started with IBM® **SmartCloud® Enterprise** (SCE), focusing on some basic use-cases and functions. We will first cover some of the popular uses before getting some hands-on experience on working with the SCE management console to perform some of the functions needed to get the services running.

This chapter also contains some hands-on exercises. For these exercises, we assume that you have already signed up and have the ability to log in to the SCE management console, as covered in the previous chapter.

Popular uses

As we discovered in *Chapter 1, IBM® SmartCloud®*, IBM® SmartCloud® Enterprise has all the fundamental capabilities required to support a broad spectrum of born-on-the-web applications for both production and non-production deployments.

This solution, developed for organizations that want a low-cost cloud environment suitable for running moderate-risk applications, can help dramatically reduce the client's IT costs. Some examples uses are as follows:

- Development and test activities
- Batch processing
- Web hosting

Features in IBM® SmartCloud® Enterprise such as pay-for-use, self-service, and rapid elasticity also enable support for use-cases in analytics, collaboration, and performance testing.

 A good set of videos on popular uses can be found on the IBM® SmartCloud® Enterprise YouTube channel at www. youtube.com/user/IBMSmartCloudEprise.

Before we see what we need to do to get one of these popular uses up and running in IBM® SmartCloud® Enterprise, let us elaborate on what we have learned in the previous chapter on the resources and look at their relationships and attributes.

Resource relationships and attributes

The following table details the full description of the available resources, their attributes, and their relationships. We can see for instance, that a volume or a persistent storage unit can be connected to a virtual machine instance during or after provisioning.

Resource	Description	Attributes and relationships
Location	The data center where the physical machines are stored	Images, instances, and SoftwareBundles are located here
Instance	An instantiation of an image into a virtual machine	The provisioning process takes an image combined with an InstanceType and optionally addresses and volumes as input, to create a running instance
InstanceType	A template for the resources associated with an Instance	Number of virtual CPUs, virtual memory, virtual local storage, and architecture (32- or 64-bit)
Address	An IP address that may be managed as an independent resource	An address may be attached to an instance. The address will always be associated with a VLAN, either public or private
VLAN	A virtual local area network	VLANs can be either public or private, only allowing a connection via a VLAN or multi-homed instance
VPN	A virtual private network	VPNs are used to securely connect to instances running in a location. A VPN connection is unique to a location
Image	A binary file that can be stored and instantiated into an instance and metadata describing it	An image is stored at a location and can be instantiated to create an instance. Public images are available at each location by default, private and shared images can be created by making a snapshot of an instance or importing an existing Image

Resource	Description	Attributes and relationships
SoftwareBundle	Installation and activation scripts and, optionally, binary files and other resources that can be installed	A SoftwareBundle can be added to an image. When that image is instantiated, the SoftwareBundle and activation scripts are injected into the instance file system
Volume	A virtual block storage device that can be used to store data and images	A volume can be attached to a VM instance during provisioning or later when it is running. The data on a volume cannot be accessed unless it is attached to an instance
Key	SSH key which is the private key should be kept by the user; the cloud makes the public key available and allows the user to generate a new key whenever needed	A key will be embedded into Linux instances during provisioning and before startup

The following figure gives a pictorial view of the relationships and their attributes as described in the previous table:

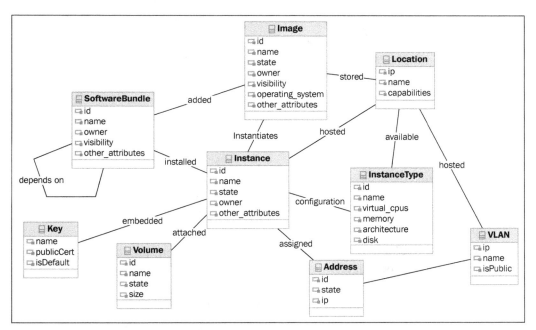

More about the resources, relationships, and attributes can be found in the developerWorks® article *Create solutions on IBM SmartCloud Enterprise: Best practices and tools* at www.ibm.com/developerworks/cloud/library/cl-smartcloudsolution1.

Now that we have a good understanding of the types, relationships, and attributes of the IBM® SmartCloud® Enterprise resources, let's get down to creating and configuring some of the resources based on an example use-case.

Provisioning our first virtual machine instance

The best way to learn is by actually doing it. Therefore, let's get some hands-on experience first. We assume that you have already signed up and have the ability to log in to the SCE management console. If not, please follow the process described in the previous chapter to get an account.

We will use the following example scenario. You want to deploy a **LAMP (Linux®, Apache™, MySQL®, PHP)** based database-driven web application called PACKT for your mostly Europe-based customers for alpha testing purposes. It must be easily reachable by the users via Internet. You do not want to lose the data in the database, and so it must be stored in some persistent storage such as the block storage described in the previous chapter.

Since you are still in the testing phase, a small virtual machine instance would suffice. As the user base is small, a system-generated-publically-accessible IP address would be acceptable.

We will next discuss how these requirements influence the choice of the resources within IBM® SmartCloud® Enterprise. We will create a virtual machine instance named PACKTinst1:

- For this instance, we want to use the latest Linux version available in the image catalog, and we already have some knowledge of Red Hat Linux. Therefore, we will base our virtual machine instance on a public image for Red Hat Enterprise 6.3 64-bit.

- As the PACKT application needs to be available from the Internet, we connect from the Internet using a system generated IP address.

- Because the application has limited requirements in terms of resources, we select the **Bronze** capacity type (2 vCPU, 4 GB vRAM, 910 GB instance storage).

- Then we mount a 60 GB persistent storage unit (volume) named PACKTvol1 to the instance.

The following figure depicts our scenario including the details we discussed previously:

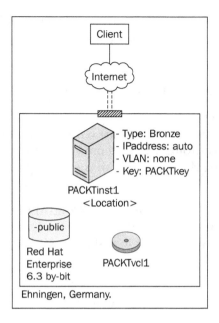

To build the example scenario, you will use the browser-based graphical SCE management console, as opposed to the command line using the **Application Programming Interface (API)**. We, therefore, start by navigating to the SCE management console, available at www.ibm.com/cloud/enterprise, where we log in using the credentials (IBM ID and password) we had configured during the ordering process in the IBM ID step in the previous chapter.

The steps to create the example scenario are as follows:

1. Create a block storage volume.
2. Create an SSH key.
3. Create a virtual machine instance.
4. Connect to the instance.
5. Configure the instance into a LAMP server and consume it.
6. Create a snapshot from this customized instance.

We will next describe each of these steps in detail.

Note that, as mentioned in the previous chapter, every time you open the SCE management console in the browser, information on scheduled maintenance windows will be displayed in the header.

This message can be closed by clicking on **Close** in the upper-right corner.

Creating a block storage volume

For this example, we will start with creating a volume which will persist after we delete the virtual machine instance. We start with the block storage volume first to show that the volume can automatically be mounted at the virtual machine instance provisioning time. Creating the volume is an easy 3-step process that can be described as follows:

1. Configure the storage by navigating to **Control Panel | Storage** and then click on **Add Storage** to get started. Select the **Data Center** (Ehningen, Germany) value that you want to instantiate (PACKTvol1), select the **Size** value (256 GB), and click on **Next**.

2. Verify the configuration and click on **Next**.

3. Read and accept the license agreement by selecting **I agree** and click on **Submit**.

When the block storage volume is created successfully, you will be prompted by a successful acknowledgement message. Next, you can continue with creating the virtual machine instance where you will specify to automatically mount this volume. But for our example, we will first create an SSH key to connect to the virtual machine instance we are about to create, which will be running a Linux operating system.

Creating an SSH key

SSH keys enable you to securely connect to your virtual machines instance(s) running a Linux operating system over the Internet.

1. Navigate to **Control Panel | Account** and then click on **Generate New Key Pair** to get started.

2. Type the name (PACKTkey) of the key pair and click on **Generate New Key Pair**.

3. Click on **Click to download key** and save the file at your local disk (the default name is **ibmcloud_<IBM ID>_rsa**).

For instances running a Windows operating system, you configure user credentials, the Administrator ID and password, during the provisioning of the request process. Find more information in the section *Connecting to the instance*.

Creating a virtual machine instance

To create a virtual machine instance, you will use a Linux operating system image from the public image catalog. To create a new instance, you need to follow an easy 4-step process:

- Select the image:
    - ○ Navigate to **Control Panel | Instance**, and then click on **Add Instance** to get started.
    - ○ To find the image you need, first select the image catalog you want to view (**Public**) and in which **Data Center** (Ehningen, Germany) you want to have the instance running. You can limit your search result by selecting 32-bit or 64-bit architecture (64-bit) and/or enter any search criteria before clicking on the **Search** button.
    - ○ Select the image that you want to instantiate (Red Hat Enterprise 6.3 (64-bit) in Ehningen, Germany) and click on **Next**.

- Configure the image:
  - ° Configure the image by at least specifying the **Request Name** value (PACKTinst1) and selecting the **Server Configuration** parameter (**Bronze 64-bit**).
  - ° Select the previously created SSH Key (PACKTkey) which we will use to connect to the instance later.
  - ° Attach the block storage volume created previously through the following steps:
    1. Click on **Add Storage.**
    2. Select the **Block Storage** volume (PACKTvol1).
    3. Check the **Mount** disk value.
    4. Type a name for the Mount point (PACKTvol1) and then click on **Add Disk.**
    5. Click on **Close.**
  - ° Validate that all the other fields contain the correct information and click on **Next**.

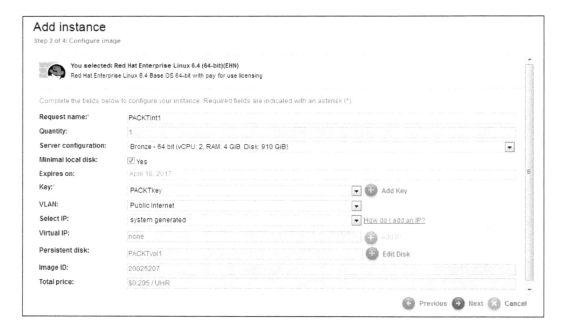

- Verify the configuration and click on **Next**.
- Read and accept the license agreement by selecting **I agree** and click on **Submit**.

When the instance is created successfully, you will be prompted with a message that lets you know you've succeeded.

After you have created the virtual machine instance, you can view its information from the **Overview** page. Once the **Status** has moved from **Requesting** and **Provisioning** to **Active**, you can access your virtual machine instance to start configuring the operating system and installing the applications.

> If you would have created a Microsoft Windows® instance, the process would be similar, though you do not need to configure an SSH key pair. You do, however, need to configure the user account you will use to connect to the instance.

Connecting to the instance

To be able to connect to an instance, you need to know how to reach it. Navigate to **Control Panel | Instance**, and click on the instance of your choice. Scroll down the page and look for either the IP address or the hostname, and copy this to paste in the connection tool later.

There are three methods for connecting to virtual machine instances running the Linux operating system and they are as follows:

*   Via SSH using the command line interface on any UNIX® based operating system such as Linux and OS X, or use PuTTY for Microsoft Windows operating system clients
*   Via SSH and a file manager on any UNIX-based operating system such as Linux and OS X, or WinSCP on Microsoft Windows clients
*   Via SSH using VNC as graphical client, available for a majority of clients

For this example, you will connect via SSH using the command line interface. To do so, start your command line interface and connect using the following command line:

```
ssh -i <keyfile> idcuser@<IPaddress>
```

Here, `<keyfile>` is the saved key during the creation of the instance, by default named ibmcloud_`<IBM ID>`_rsa (for example, `ibmcloud_john.doe@uk.ibm.com_rsa`) and `<IPaddress>` is the IP address of the instance.

Microsoft Windows operating system clients connecting to Linux virtual machine instances, as mentioned before, can use tools such as PuTTY. This, however, requires some intermediate steps using `PuttyGen.exe` to convert the RSA keyfile into the PuTTY format. Details on how to do this can be found in both the User's Guide and demonstration video #2 at the end of this chapter.

 Users can connect to the Windows virtual machine instances using a Remote Desktop Client application running on their client machines. This application uses the **Remote Desktop Protocol (RDP)**. RDP clients are available for Windows, Linux, and OS X® operating systems.

Configuring and consuming the instance

Naturally, as you would do for any newly installed operating system, you need to make sure that the entire server is properly hardened: patches have been applied, security settings are according to the requirements, and proper logging is configured. The hardening process should also include setting up the monitoring and backup/ restore options. Options like this will be covered in *Chapter 4, Advanced Use-cases*.

Once you have hardened the virtual machine instance's operating system, you can start installing and configuring your Apache, PHP, and MySQL applications and configure your database files to reside on the block storage volume. This, however, is not different from any traditional server configuration, and so we will not spend more time on this as we have covered all the steps related to cloud computing.

Creating a snapshot from the customized instance

Now that you have your instance up and running, you may want to make sure that you capture your work for restoring later on. This will save you the time you needed to install and configure the virtual machine instance the first time. The way you do this is by taking a snapshot of the instance created earlier. IBM® SmartCloud® Enterprise offers three native options to create an image, each with its own unique characteristics.

The main difference between the three options is the flexibility that you have in being able to suit just one or multiple use-cases using a single image. As an example, if you are able to include all the changes you performed during the hardening of your example instance, while being able to parameterize the installation of the applications on top, you are very flexible in creating new instances for different applications using the same image. The options are as follows, listed from the least flexible to the most flexible:

- Take a snapshot of the instance
- Customize an image by adding extra parameters
- Leverage scripts to automatically configure and deploy middleware after provisioning, using the **Rapid Deployment Service (RDS)** provided by IBM

Each of these three options will be discussed in the following sections.

Next to these three native options, there is a fourth option. This option uses software that is provided as an image in the IBM® SmartCloud® Enterprise public image catalog, which is called the Image Construction and Composition Tool. This software helps you in creating an image based on building blocks called bundles.

Taking a snapshot of the instance

This basic option allows you to create an image from a virtual machine instance that you have been running to create replica instances. This option is triggered by using the **Create an image** function from the SCE management console or by using the corresponding API calls.

Note that the snapshot of an instance also contains the IP address. If you want to create more than one instance from the same image, you will also need to reconfigure the IP address.

As mentioned earlier, this option is the least flexible because all the instances created from the new image are exactly the same. But for the example scenario, this is exactly what you need. So, let's see which actions you have to perform to create an image from your previously created virtual machine instance:

1. Select an image by navigating to **Control Panel | Instance**, and selecting the instance (PACKTinst) you want to create an image from. Click on **Create private image** to get started.

2. Configure the private image. Specify the **Name** (PACKTinst1 image) you want and click on **Submit**.

When the image is successfully configured, you will be prompted with a message that lets you know you've succeeded.

Creating a snapshot from an instance may take up to an hour to process, and will stop the instance in the process. Once the image has been created, the status will be updated in **Control Panel | Images**.

Customizing an image by adding extra parameters

After taking a snapshot of an instance, you can modify the files in the created image to automatically generate a new screen during provisioning, asking for any additional parameters you might need, to use the image more flexibly. This will allow you to, for example, ask for a username and password for the Apache software installation that you want to do automatically after the provisioning process.

The image configuration files we need to edit for this are stored in the Asset Catalog. From there, you can modify the `parameters.xml` file to include `<field>` tags of your choice in order to include the additional parameters that you require. Once the `<field>` tags are included, you will we be prompted with an additional screen asking for an input every time you provision a virtual machine instance. Following is an example of a `<field>` tag which will request for the parameter `userPassword` that needs to comply to a regular expression string as well:

```
<field name="userPassword" label="User Password" type="password"
pattern="^\w*(?=\w*\d)(?=\w*[a-z])(?=\w*[A-Z])\w*$"
patternErrorMessage="Invalid Password. Must contain at least 1 number, at
least 1 lower case letter, and at least 1 upper case letter.">
</field>
```

More details about this technique can be found in the developerWorks article *Parameterize cloud images for custom instances on the fly* at www.ibm.com/developerworks/cloud/library/cl-parameterizecloudimages.

Using rapid deployment services

An alternative to the previous two options is to use RDS, which enables you to further customize images in the catalog automatically, by installing and configuring middleware after provisioning. This technique uses build-scripts, which can be uploaded in the image. The image, as mentioned previously, is stored in the Asset Catalog.

Once the build-scripts have been added to the image, they will be copied to the instance during the provisioning process. This is done through the `activation_script` directory. The build-scripts will be launched in the newly created instance through a startup script.

RDS leverages **Simple Product Installation** (**SPiN**), an IBM scripting language that is platform-agnostic. With RDS, highly customizable and complex assets can be quickly deployed with minimum specialist intervention; the automation features of RDS reduce the number of human errors that can occur during installation.

More information about this technique can be found in the developerWorks article *Deploy products using rapid deployment service* available at `www.ibm.com/developerworks/cloud/library/cl-rdsassetoncloud`.

Many more functions!

This chapter has only touched upon what is possible with IBM® SmartCloud® Enterprise. We covered the basic functions of the SCE management console to provision different types of resources and secured our work by configuring the instance by creating a snapshot of it.

More information about the SCE management console can be found in the User's guide and demonstration videos in the video library, both described in the following section.

User's guide

Step-by-step instructions for all the basic functions can be found in the **User's Guide** page which can be found on the **Support** page of the SCE management console. This 100+ pages essential guide to getting started with IBM® SmartCloud® Enterprise and IBM® SmartCloud® Enterprise Application Services covers the following areas:

- Provides an overview of IBM® SmartCloud® Enterprise and IBM® SmartCloud® Application Services

- Provides information about the user interface (SCE management console)

- Provides information about connecting, configuring, and managing your Linux operating system's virtual machine instances

- Provides information about connecting, configuring, and managing your Windows operating system's virtual machine instances

- Provides answers to the frequently asked questions

- Provides the frequently asked questions

- Provides appendices on accessibility and abbreviations

Demonstration videos

As mentioned in the previous chapter, the **Video Library** option on the **Support** page of the SCE management console offers very useful demonstrations and instructions. These demonstration videos can be found in the **SmartCloud Enterprise Demos** playlist of the IBM® SmartCloud® Enterprise YouTube channel, which also contains other popular videos, at `www.youtube.com/user/IBMSmartCloudEprise`.

The videos, on average between 4-6 minutes long, allow you to quickly get educated on a specific subject by seeing the actions being performed.

IBM® SmartCloud® Enterprise

The following videos on IBM® SmartCloud® Enterprise are available:

- Instance creation and management
- Connecting to an instance using an SSH client
- Working with IP, storage, and keys
- User roles and administration
- Image creation and instance creation
- Setting up the Firewalls
- Establishing a virtual LAN
- Working with the Asset Catalog
- Sharing private images and creating support forums
- VM dedicated Firewall
- Creating service offerings and service instances
- Bundles and extending images

IBM® SmartCloud® Application Services

The list of videos also extends to IBM® SmartCloud® Application Services, covered in more details in *Chapter 6*, *Further Developments*:

- DevOps scenario
- Portability between IBM® SmartCloud® Application Services (public cloud solution) and IBM PureApplications (private cloud solution)
- How to install, set up, and use the IBM Workload Deployer® RAD plugin on IBM® SmartCloud®
- Create a step-by-step simple pattern type with IBM® SmartCloud® Application Workload Services
- Enabling Tivoli® monitoring shared service on IBM® SmartCloud® Application Services

Summary

In this chapter, we have learned how to get started using IBM® SmartCloud® Enterprise. Before we started building hands-on experience by provisioning both a block storage volume and a virtual machine instance, we covered the resource model including the attributes and relationships.

We also learned how to create a snapshot of an instance to secure our work and allow future reuse. Lastly, we covered the various sources of information that offer valuable instructions and demonstrations to get educated on them even more.

In the next chapter, we will learn some of the more advanced configuration options to support more diverse use-cases in detail, taking your knowledge of IBM® SmartCloud® Enterprise to the next level.

4

Advanced Use-cases

This chapter covers advanced functions, which go one step deeper that the use-cases and functions covered in *Chapter 2, IBM® SmartCloud® Enterprise*, and *Chapter 3, Getting Started*. First let's merge the concepts showed in the figures in afore mentioned chapters into one figure containing them all, as the following figure depicts.

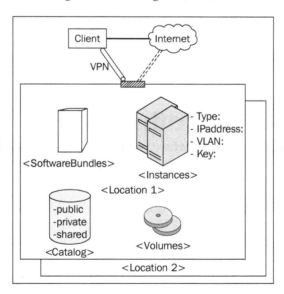

From the preceding figure we can see that applications with high availability requirements ultimately need to be run in two data centers. This in turn means that we need to make sure that all resources we need are available at two locations:

- We need to arrange network connections to both locations, as network access methods are unique to a location
- The images are also unique to a location, so we need to copy our private and shared images to every location where we might need them
- Lastly, block storage volumes (persistent storage units) are unique to a location but can be mounted from a different location as well

To be able to provide you with an overview of how advanced use-cases are supported, we will do a deep dive into the following subjects in this chapter:

- Using the REST (and other) APIs
- Image management
- Securing our resources
- Backup and restore options
- Monitoring instances
- High availability and redundancy

Using REST (and other) APIs

The **Application Programming Interface (API)** services for IBM® SmartCloud® Enterprise provides you with the ability to manage your instances by using third-party applications. As the heading suggests, different APIs are available for this.

- The first building block of the APIs is the REST API; it is flexible and simple to use, and implements clients for providing **Representational State Transfer (REST)** based endpoints. The REST API can be used for applications such as JAX-WS, SOA, XUL, and cURL.
- Second, there is the **Java API** which is a wrapper around the REST API; each Java API method calls the REST API in turn.
- Lastly there is the **Command Line Interface (CLI)** API which is ideal for scripting languages such as Shell and PERL. The CLI API calls the Java API, which in turn calls the REST API.

The following figure depicts the different APIs and their interdependence.

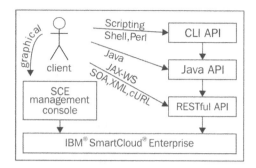

User guides and references

Each of the different APIs also has a user guide of its own; all are available through the **Support** tab of the SCE management console as well as in the **Asset Catalog**:

- The REST API is described in the **API User Guide** (also known as REST API Reference) which focuses on these REST-based endpoints. IBM makes available tools that can be used by the customers to enable use of APIs with the Services.

- The **Java REST API Client** archive contains examples and references for using Java applications to communicate with IBM® SmartCloud® Enterprise.

- The CLI API is described in the **Command Line Tool Reference Guide** which provides necessary details on the current command-line tool for developers and architects working with IBM® SmartCloud® Enterprise.

Additionally there is an **Asset Catalog** entry named **Certificates for the IBM SmartCloud Enterprise API**, which explains how to work with HTTPS certificates. This guide gives an example of how to use the API in an IBM WebSphere® J2EE environment.

Provisioning a virtual machine instance using the REST API

To make it more practical, let's use the REST API to provision a virtual machine instance as we did in *Chapter 3, Getting Started,* using the SCE management console. For the example we will follow parts of an example scenario described in the API User Guide as well.

The <base_URL>

The REST API accesses resources using a unique uniform resource identifier (URI) built from the <base_URL> by using the standard set of HTTP Methods. The <base_URL> incorporates an API version number to make sure that you call the API version you expect. This version number is appended at the end of the <base_URL>. Check the API User Guide for the current <base_URL>, which is at (at the time of writing):

```
www-147.ibm.com/computecloud/enterprise/api/rest/20100331
```

The REST API service for IBM® SmartCloud® Enterprise is a secured web resource which uses basic authentication. In order to use the API services, you must be registered with IBM® SmartCloud® Enterprise and provide your credentials when prompted. All requests to the API are required to be done via HTTPS, which will ensure transport level encryption.

Using the REST API in a browser

When you want to experiment with the REST API, the easiest thing to do is use a browser. This will allow you to explore the API and understand the data returned. However, in general it is not possible to access the IBM® SmartCloud® Enterprise REST API with a browser because the API is configured to scan the HTTP header and block most client browsers as it assumes that only scripts or applications access it.

We can, however, simply modify the User Agent HTTP header of the browser, which will allow you to use a browser. Second, you will use a RESTclient browser add-on to make the interaction with the API easier to follow. The following two sections take you through the steps needed to modify the User Agent HTTP header and install the RESTclient.

For our example we use the Mozilla® Firefox® browser and add-ons.

User Agent Switcher

To be able to modify the User Agent HTTP header of the browser using Firefox, you install the Firefox User Agent Switcher add-on which can be found at addons.mozilla.org/en-US/firefox/addon/user-agent-switcher and installed by using the **Add to Firefox** button.

After having installed the add-on you need to configure a new User Agent Profile to fit our needs. You add a new User Agent Profile using the Edit User Agents dialog, found at **Tools | Default User Agent** (note that this name shows the User Agent you have selected). Use `Cloud API` as **Description** and `cloudapi` as **User Agent**, leaving the other fields to their default value.

> Remember to set the User Agent HTTP header back to normal when you are finished exploring the IBM® SmartCloud® Enterprise REST API.

RESTClient

After having installed the User Agent Switcher, you will install an additional Firefox add-on to make it easier for us to interact with the REST API using a browser. For this you will install a Firefox add-on called RESTClient, a debugger for REST web services, but any add-on or other tool of preference can be used.

This add-on can be found at `addons.mozilla.org/en-US/firefox/addon/restclient` and installed by using the **Add to Firefox** button. Once installed, you:

- Set a custom header with **Name** `Content-Type` and **Value** `application/x-www-form-urlencoded`

- Set the basic authentication to the **Username** and **Password** which you have set during ordering and have used already in *Chapter 3, Getting Started*

> More methods for using the REST API such as using with Linux® cURL and Java can be found in the Thoughts on Cloud blog post at `thoughtsoncloud.com/index.php/2011/11/introduction-to-the-restful-api-of-ibm-smartcloud-enterprise`.

Creating a virtual machine instance using the API

Now you have installed the needed Firefox add-ons for you to interact with the REST API you can create a virtual machine instance similar to what you have done in *Chapter 3, Getting Started*. But before you can create our virtual machine instance, you must find all the information that is needed to create the instance.

You will use the following procedure to gather the information you need to create a virtual machine instance. At the end of the procedure you will use the gathered information and create a virtual machine instance using the REST API:

1. Select a unique user-friendly name for the instance that you are planning to create. To verify if the name is not assigned to any existing instance, use:

   ```
   GET <base_URL>/instances
   ```

2. Generate an SSH key pair to log on to your Linux instance later.
   Use the command:

   ```
   POST <base_URL>/keys
   ```

3. Select a Linux (RHEL 6.3) image from which you want to create an instance. Use this command to list all images offered:

   ```
   GET <base_URL>/offerings/image
   ```

4. The response (part of) that it we will get looks like this:

   ```
   ...
   <Image>
      <ImageID>20025207</ImageID>
         <Name>Red Hat Enterprise Linux 6.3</Name>
   ...
   ```

5. Select instance type for the instance. Use this command to get the list of instance types for the image, using the `<ImageID>` from previous step:

   ```
   GET <base_URL>/offerings/image/<imageID>
   ```

6. The response (part of it) that we will get looks like this:

   ```
   ...
   <SupportedInstanceTypes>
      <InstanceType>
         <ID>CMP-COPPER-32.1/2048/60</ID>
            <Label>Copper 32 bit</Label>
   ...
   ```

7. Select the data center onto which you want to host your instance. Use this command to get a list of the available data centers:

   ```
   GET <base_URL>/locations
   ```

8. The response (part of it) that we will get looks like this:

   ```
   ...
   <Location>
      <ID>61</ID>
         <Name>Ehningen, Germany</Name>
   ...
   ```

9. View the details of a specific location using:

```
GET <base_URL>/locations/<location_ID>
```

10. Select an additional storage volume that you want to attach to the instance. Use this command to obtain the information about our volumes:

```
GET <base_URL>/storage
```

11. You must check the state of the persistent storage volume to verify whether it can be attached to the instance we are creating using the command:

```
GET <base_URL>/storage/<Storage_ID>
```

12. After you have obtained all the details (required and optional) for creating instance, you can create the new instance from that image using the POST command:

```
POST <base_URL>/offerings/image Name=PACKTsvr2&ImageID=20025207&
InstanceType=CMP-COPPER-32.1/2048/60&Location=61&
```

13. For the instance to be usable it has to be in ACTIVE state. It takes a short time to boot the instance even after the instance is provisioned. To check the status of the instance use this command, where <instance_ID> is the ID returned from the POST command:

```
GET <base_URL>/instances/<instance_ID>
```

14. Find the instance name and IP address of the machine to log on to the instance using the command:

```
GET <base_URL>/instances/<instance_ID>
```

Once you have our virtual machine instance successfully provisioned and know the IP address, you can connect to it using the same mechanism as described in *Chapter 3*, *Getting Started*, and continue with hardening and installing the application(s) you require.

Powerful API functionalities

As the previous example shows, you can use the APIs to create new virtual machine instance using only one POST command. This allows you to highly automate your interaction with IBM® SmartCloud® Enterprise using any scripting language of choice. But the APIs are even more powerful than the SCE management console in two ways.

Firstly the APIs allow you to use advanced parameters such as **anti-collocation** to make sure that our two virtual machine instances do not run on the same physical hardware to account for hardware failure. Another powerful API functionality is **guest messaging**, which allows you to receive and retrieve status messages from our virtual machine instance.

Secondly, the APIs allow you to use tools such as the **deployment utility tool**, which offers us a graphical interface with many powerful features to make full use of the APIs. Examples of this are automating parallel creation requests and acting as single management dashboard for all our IBM® SmartCloud® Enterprise resources.

Let's look at each of these functionalities one by one in the following sections.

Anti-collocation

When you're building a highly available architecture — for instance a clustered application utilizing two virtual machine instances — you want to make sure that both virtual machine instances are running on different physical servers. When you use the anti-collocation parameter for your two virtual machine instances, you ensure that the overall availability of the clustered application will not be impacted when a physical hardware fails.

To use the parameter, specify the instance ID of the virtual machine instance you want the newly created virtual machine instance to be physically separated from. If you do not specify any instance ID, then the newly created instance may be provisioned at any physical location.

```
antiCollocationInstance (-- Anti-collocation_instanceID)
```

For now it is only possible to manage two instances, and anti-collocation currently supports the segregation of physical hosts but does guarantee network switch individuality/uniqueness.

More information about this parameter can be found in the API User Guide.

Guest messaging

This new functionality provides a set of API calls to monitor the health of your virtual machine instances. Guest messaging has been implemented to allow IBM® SmartCloud® Enterprise applications, the IBM® SmartCloud® Application Services as detailed in *Chapter 6*, *Further Developments*, to communicate with the underlying virtual machine instances. With guest messaging the virtual machine instances send periodic status messages to the application.

You can enable the guest message forward feature during creation of our virtual machine instance with the parameters added to the POST method.

```
messageForward (-- messageForward true|false)
```

These guest messages can also be retrieved from the virtual machine instance using the API to get the latest status as well as a historical perspective. When using the API you receive <n> of guest messages and their timestamps from your virtual machine.

```
GET <base_URL>/instances/<instance_ID>
/guestMessage?messageNumber=<n>
```

 The guest message forward feature cannot be dynamically enabled or disabled after an instance is provisioned. Windows® operating system instances do not support the guest forward feature, only newly created Linux instances support the feature.

The deployment utility tool

The deployment utility tool, developed by IBM cloud architect Dominique Vernier but not part of IBM® SmartCloud® Enterprise, allows you to deploy complex infrastructure topologies and manage our resources with ease.

This tool allows you to provision multiple resources (a topology) on IBM® SmartCloud® Enterprise based using a single deployment file. Normally when you want to do this, you might need to spend quite some time using the SCE management console planning the order in which you create your resources. Only think back to the example environment in *Chapter 3, Getting Started*, where you first created the block storage volume before creating the virtual machine instance to allow the volume to be mounted automatically.

Using this tool you describe all the resources you need in a single deployment file and launch this deployment file from the deployment utility tool. The tool automatically arranges the order in which the resource created based on their dependencies of each resource. The tool can also, when the dependencies allow this, launch multiple creation requests in parallel, to speed-up the total deployment time.

Lastly, the tool also allows you to directly manage IBM® SmartCloud® Enterprise resources from a single interface as the following screenshot depicts:

More information can be found in the the developerWorks® article *Deploy a complex topology* at www.ibm.com/developerworks/cloud/library/cl-clouddeployutility and the **Asset Catalog** entry of the latest version of the deployment utility linked in the article.

Image management

As you have learned in previous chapters, every virtual machine instance is based on an image from the image catalog. This catalog already contains public images, but can also be extended with private and shared images as well. In *Chapter 3, Getting Started*, we already covered the three standard options for creating private images: taking a snapshot of an instance, customizing an image by adding extra parameters, and relying on the Rapid Deployment Service.

Next to these three native options there are also public images available in the image catalog that contains third-party software solutions to create or import images. In this section we will extend your knowledge on image management in IBM® SmartCloud® Enterprise, specifically focusing on private and shared images. In *Chapter 5, There's an Ecosystem for That*, we will specifically focus on public images in the catalog.

Creating dynamic virtual images

As opposed to the three more static images creation options mentioned previously — which all still require you to perform manual configuration steps after the instance has been created — wouldn't it be great if you could use fully dynamic virtual images?

The foundation of dynamic virtual images is the inclusion of a special set of activation scripts, performing dynamic configuration activities that need to occur for every deployment of the image. Examples of this are updating the IP address, performing configuration actions on previously installed software, and installing application content.

IBM Image Construction and Composition Tool

One of the third-party solutions to create dynamic images, and also create and import images into IBM® SmartCloud® Enterprise, is called the **IBM Image Construction and Composition Tool (ICCT)**. This solution helps you to create an image based on building blocks called bundles. The general idea behind it is to create reusable assets, by bundling software configuration files with images, creating dynamic virtual images.

A good place to start to understand both the concept of dynamic virtual images and the basics of ICCT is the developerWorks article *Establish a system to build custom virtual cloud images* at www.ibm.com/developerworks/cloud/library/ cl-buildcloudimageICCT. Additionally there is a thorough deep dive into the capabilities of ICCT in a four-part developerWorks article series which consists of:

1. **Create software bundles for VMs with ICCT**: In this article you will see how to create software bundles for virtual machine instances, create and set up ICCT on IBM® SmartCloud® Enterprise, and retrieve and update software bundles, which is available at www.ibm.com/developerworks/cloud/ library/cl-bundlemanage1.

2. **Use and maintain software bundles with ICCT**: This article tells you how to create a custom image with the software bundle created in Part 1 available at www.ibm.com/developerworks/cloud/library/cl-bundlemanage2.

3. **Clone and modify an asset for customized provisioning**: It tells you how to customize an image by cloning and modifying a Rational Asset Manager (RAM) asset and it is available at www.ibm.com/developerworks/cloud/ library/cl-bundlemanage3.

4. **Create images with ICCT**: This article describes the three mechanisms to create images using ICCT to capture a customized image and the mechanism to manually add a dependency between an image and a software bundle by updating the semantic topology file. It is available at `www.ibm.com/developerworks/cloud/library/cl-bundlemanage4`.

One of the powerful features of the ICCT is that its mechanism is built to work with many cloud services including IBM® SmartCloud® Enterprise. The tool can, therefore, also be used to provision instances consistently across multiple different cloud services.

This is specifically useful for cloudbursting—creating additional resources on a secondary cloud service when the primary cloud service has reached full capacity—or cloudsourcing—for instance when you run an application in a public cloud service during development and testing, and in a private cloud service during quality assurance and production because of the sensitivity of the data contained in the application.

Last but not least, ICCT is now integrated with the IBM® SmartCloud® Enterprise Application Workload Service which allows us to create custom virtual images and deploy those images with IBM® SmartCloud® Enterprise Application Services, the PureApplication™ System, or IBM Workload Deployer. This new functionality enhances the interoperability between IBM's public and private clouds services and gives you additional choice and flexibility in virtual image deployment. Read *Chapter 6, Further Developments* for more information.

CohesiveFT

Another solution that allows you to create dynamic images is Cohesive Flexible Technologies' Elastic Server™. This solution builds custom images and software packages with a simple user interface, which makes it another great way to create your own custom images. Elastic Server is an also available image in the IBM® SmartCloud® Enterprise image catalog.

Although the Smart Elastic Server solution is designed for easy customization of Red Hat and SUSE Linux images, a wide variety of images can be customized and uploaded to the IBM® SmartCloud® Enterprise environment. This Thoughts on Cloud blog post takes us through the basics of creating an image using Smart Elastic Server:

`thoughtsoncloud.com/index.php/2012/02/creating-custom-images-on-ibm-smartcloud-enterprise`

Importing images

Apart from creating static or dynamic images, you can also import images into the IBM® SmartCloud® Enterprise image catalog. To do so there are, again, a wide variety of options available: there are default options available or we can use third-party solutions.

Next, we will cover these and an additional use-case for moving images between locations.

Default features

Since the release of Version 2.0 of IBM® SmartCloud® Enterprise images in the open source image format, OVA can be imported. You can import Linux images into our image catalog, saving time and effort to recreate servers running elsewhere in IBM® SmartCloud® Enterprise. It also allows us to import appliance images, which cannot be rebuild at all. The default feature Windows Import/Copy allows you to import Windows Server virtual images from an existing environment into IBM® SmartCloud® Enterprise.

How to import an image into IBM® SmartCloud® Enterprise is clearly explained in the document **Creating and Customizing Images and Software Bundles** available on the **Support** page of the SCE management console. Another source of information, specifically on importing Linux images, is this developerWorks article:

`www.ibm.com/developerworks/cloud/library/cl-importlinuxOSimage`

CohesiveFT

CohesiveFT, previously mentioned for its image creation features, can also be used to import images into IBM® SmartCloud® Enterprise, solving the migration issues when moving to cloud. Read more at `thoughtsoncloud.com/index.php/2012/05/extending-the-cloud-ecosystem-data-center-to-ibm-smartcloud-enterprise-migration`.

Transfering images between different accounts

As we have learned in *Chapter 3, Getting Started,* each private image is unique to, and therefore only visible using, a single account. When you want a private image to be available in another account—for instance when a single client has more than one account for different purposes such as development, test, quality assurance, or production—you need to be able to transfer the images between those accounts.

Read the step-by-step guide to transfer an image from one account to another. One prerequisite for this task is that the operator has to have the credentials for both accounts.

`www.ibm.com/developerworks/cloud/library/cl-smartcloudsolution2`

Delivering images

Take the value of IBM® SmartCloud® Enterprise one step further by allowing others to utilize your created services. IBM® SmartCloud® Enterprise offers users this option — to design and create their own PaaS services — next to the readily available platform services in IBM® SmartCloud® Application Services. See more on the pre-build platform services in *Chapter 6, Further Developments*.

The possibility to create your own PaaS services is implemented by the **Cloud Services Framework**, which is intended to make it easier for customers and partners to create and deliver services on top of IBM® SmartCloud® Enterprise. Now you can quickly and easily define and register all the aspects of your service and make it available to your end customers.

To fully understand what the Cloud Services Framework has to offer read the developerWorks article *SmartCloud Cloud Services Framework, Part 1: Create a mashup service*. This article allows you to learn how to create and register a mashup service in IBM® SmartCloud® Enterprise and is available at `www.ibm.com/developerworks/cloud/library/cl-servicesmashup1`.

Securing your resources

When placing your applications and data in cloud services, the security of our resources and assets becomes a top priority. With the introduction of cloud computing, new security concerns emerged, such as how to deal with the security of highly virtualized environments. More specifically, how can you secure your virtual machine instances from targeted threats and attacks, and protect your data in a rapid provisioning and de-provisioning environment.

To provide more insight into these new challenges, IBM has written this paper to enable discussion around the new security challenges that cloud introduces and how these are addressed by IBM's cloud offerings. Read the white paper *How does IBM deliver cloud security* for more information, which is available for download at `www-935.ibm.com/services/be/en/attachments/pdf/2012_05_23_3728_Cloud_Security_How_does_IBM_D.pdf`

Secondly there is a developerWorks article that highlights some of the security topics that need to be considered when provisioning virtual machine instances in IBM® SmartCloud® Enterprise. This article acts as a good starting point for the detailed security sections that will follow:

`www.ibm.com/developerworks/cloud/library/cl-cloudvmsecurityrisks`

Lastly, security is not only about fencing your assets and data. Being in control of the security of your resources and data requires insight; knowing when your assets are showing usage patters outside the normal pattern and being able to act on this is essential. This is why monitoring is one of the security sections.

ISO 27001 certification

As mentioned in *Chapter 2, IBM® SmartCloud® Enterprise*, IBM® SmartCloud® Enterprise has obtained certification to information security standard ISO 27001. This further enhances the security standards used and the protection features offered. The ISO (International Organization for Standardization) 27001 standard provides a framework to ensure that the certified organization addresses security needs for its customers. The certification from Bureau Veritas was attained for all IBM® SmartCloud® Services data centers.

To review the entire list, please visit the IBM ISO Management System Certifications website at `www-935.ibm.com/services/us/en/it-services/iso-management-system-certifications.html`.

Network security

As IBM® SmartCloud® Enterprise, like any other public cloud service, is accessible via the network, we need to make sure that this is done securely to conform to our security requirements. In this section we will discuss some of the network security options available. To start with, all IBM® SmartCloud® Services data centers are equipped with Secure Shield Internet connectivity that includes features such as:

- Additional firewall and intrusion protection
- New distributed denial of service protection
- New Botnet protection
- Updates to hypervisor and additional level of isolation

Network concepts and tools

Additional information on how to implement VPNs and VLANs, as briefly covered in *Chapter 2, IBM® SmartCloud® Enterprise*, developerWorks article *Networking Concepts and Tools for IBM® SmartCloud® Enterprise* guides you through all the important concepts of networking for IBM® SmartCloud® Enterprise. The article also explains how to use network tools including OpenSSH, OpenVPN, and proxy servers to set up different network topologies and solve connectivity problems, giving examples important to common cloud situations. This article can be found at www.ibm.com/developerworks/cloud/library/cl-networkingtools.

Additionally there is developerWorks article on how to *Set up a highly available firewall and load balancer in the IBM cloud* that elaborates on the options to not only configure firewalls to secure our assets, but also to do this in a high available configuration to prevent single points of failure. This article can be found at www.ibm.com/developerworks/cloud/library/cl-setupfirewalloncloud.

Integrating your authentication policy using a proxy

Managing business rules for the authorization and authentication of custom-built cloud applications in IBM® SmartCloud® Enterprise doesn't have to be a difficult task. In the following developerWorks article's URL, you learn how to build business rules into a proxy that bridge among the CLI-, Java-, and REST APIs. Using a proxy also keeps users from skipping around your business rules when accessing the SCE management console.

www.ibm.com/developerworks/cloud/library/cl-cloudtip-authproxy

Host security

Once the network access is secured, you can look at host security. In short, this covers how to secure your virtual machine instances with data security and data protection features.

Hypervisor security

Since the release of Version 1.2 of IBM® SmartCloud® Enterprise the **Mandatory Access Control (MAC)** in the **Kernel-based Virtual Machine (KVM)** hypervisor has been enabled. This adds an additional level of isolation against guest breakouts; where a virtual machine instance could potentially attack its host system.

For more information on guest breakout prevention and other KVM security information see the white paper *KVM: Hypervisor Security You Can Depend On* at `www-01.ibm.com/common/ssi/cgi-bin/ssialias?infotype=SA&subtype=WH&htm lfid=LXW03004USEN`.

Encrypting data in virtual machine instances

Encrypting the filesystem above the hypervisor is a way to secure data-at-rest and to provide assurance that others can't access the data.

The following developerWorks article's URL demonstrates some technologies and applications that you can use to encrypt data inside virtual machine instances. It shows how to encrypt a block storage volume and how to encrypt the home directory. This article takes you through these scenarios:

- Encrypt a block storage volume on Linux using dm-crypt
- Encrypt a block storage volume on Windows Server using the Windows Encrypting File System (EFS)
- Encrypt a home directory on Linux using Enterprise Cryptographic Filesystem (eCryptfs)

The article is available at `www.ibm.com/developerworks/cloud/library/cl-sce-encryptdata`.

A second developerWorks article details how to set up data encryption on your Windows virtual machine instance using these scenarios:

- Full disk encryption using TrueCrypt
- Encrypt a block storage volume using BitLocker
- Encrypt files and folder using the Windows Encrypting File System (EFS).
- Encrypt the swap file using fsutil.

This article is available at `www.ibm.com/developerworks/cloud/library/cl-scedataencryption-windows`.

Backup and restore options

IBM® SmartCloud® Enterprise offers you a great flexibility in the options and possibilities, which can increase our time to market significantly. Nothing, however, comes without a price. In this case the flexibility comes at the price of you managing everything above the hypervisor yourself. You, therefore, need to think of basic IT necessities, as any other IT environment would need, such as a reliable backup/restore solution.

While some users prefer to use their existing backup solutions running outside an IBM® SmartCloud® Enterprise data center, others prefer to configure a virtual machine instance with an automated backup solution. Let's look at some of the options in the next section.

Backup using the storage capabilities

Virtual machine instance can be backed up—taken a snapshot of—using one of the options to create an image of it as covered in *Chapter 3, Getting Started*. But which options are there to take backup/restore one step further, either or both automating the backup of your virtual instances and creating a backup to an off-site location?

There are many choices for backing up your data using the capabilities of IBM® SmartCloud® Enterprise:

- You can use any of these storage types to backup—copy—your data on file level, either manually scripted or using automated backup software.

- Additionally you can also clone block storage volumes to the same or a different IBM® SmartCloud® Enterprise location, as you can do with images.

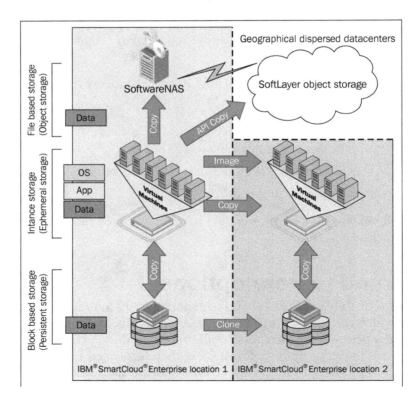

More in-depth information on these possibilities can be found in developerWorks article *Recover data in IBM SmartCloud Enterprise* at `www.ibm.com/developerworks/cloud/library/cl-datarecovery`.

Monitoring instances

As mentioned earlier, securing the perimeter and data is the key. Knowing what is going on in real-time is equally important. Let's look at some of the options that you have, to monitor your instances, apart from the afore mentioned deployment utility tool which also offers a monitoring dashboard for our virtual machine instances and other assets.

IBM Tivoli® Monitoring

Using IBM Tivoli® software to monitor your IBM® SmartCloud® Enterprise services can be either done by using a pre-build image for the task such as Tivoli® Monitoring, or installed manually inside or outside an IBM® SmartCloud® Enterprise location.

Using IBM Tivoli® Monitoring, you can monitor virtual machine resources and trigger a variety of automated actions — such as sending alert messages or provisioning virtual machines — based on the results. Find more information in the developerWorks article Monitor IBM® SmartCloud® Enterprise virtual machines with IBM Tivoli Monitoring at `www.ibm.com/developerworks/cloud/library/cl-monitorcloudvms-tivoli`.

Alternatively you can also use a **Software as a service (SaaS)** solution such as Tivoli Live-monitoring services, ready to use right from the cloud. Find out more at `www-935.ibm.com/services/us/en/it-services/tivoli-live-monitoring-services.html`.

Managing from a mobile device

Managing your IBM® SmartCloud® Enterprise resources right from your mobile device allows you to stay in control whenever and wherever. The following *Thoughts on Cloud* blog post takes you through a set of technology previews that allow you to do exactly that.

Additionally, the solution also allows you to download and e-mail command output and logs from running virtual machine instances, and record instance expiration time to your calendar. With this capability, you can share information about your cloud resources with colleagues.

The article is available at thoughtsoncloud.com/index.php/2012/08/manage-and-monitor-ibm-smartcloud-resources-from-your-mobile-device.

High availability

Single instance configurations will not cover all your requirements for high availability and redundancy, as is the case in traditional IT environments as well. Defining a valid architecture to support your requirements is a vital element in making sure that your configuration will be able to perform according to the service level agreements you need to support. The developerWorks article *High availability apps in the IBM Cloud* details how to protect a cloud-enabled, production-grade application against single points of failure and, like this book does, takes you through some examples as well. Find the article at www.ibm.com/developerworks/cloud/library/cl-highavailabilitycloud.

Additionally, IBM® SmartCloud® Enterprise offers specific features such as the ability to configure multiple IP addresses, private VLANs, and anti-collocation of virtual machine instances, in case we are building more sophisticated configurations than just a single virtual machine instance, such as a layered web server architecture. See the network security section for the network features and the API section for the anti-collocation parameter.

Summary

In this chapter we have learned the most commonly used advanced functions and features of IBM® SmartCloud® Enterprise, covering the powerful APIs including a step-by-step example to get some hands-on experience. Next we covered the concept of image management and saw the options to create dynamic virtual images followed by some of the best practices on how to handle security on multiple layers.

Halfway through the chapter, we covered means to back up data and monitor your resources to get a grip on what your resources are doing. Lastly, we briefly covered high availability and redundancy options.

In the next chapter, we will cover the public catalog images available in IBM® SmartCloud® Enterprise, to learn about the out of the box functionality available.

5
There's an Ecosystem for That

In *Chapter 1, IBM® SmartCloud®*, we covered the IBM® SmartCloud® portfolio and learned what IBM has to offer in terms of cloud computing solutions. *Chapter 2* to *Chapter 4* covered more specifically what IBM® SmartCloud® Enterprise has to offer, where we have seen that it offers rapid provisioned, self-service, elastic, and on demand infrastructure services in a pay-for-use model. But wouldn't it be great if you would be able to extend these infrastructure services with an application stack that, just as fast, delivers the functionality that you require — without having to install the application yourself?

In *Chapter 2, IBM® SmartCloud® Enterprise*, we already briefly covered that IBM® SmartCloud® Enterprise has the ability to create and upload your own images in the image catalog, which we detailed in *Chapter 3, Getting Started* and *Chapter 4, Advanced Use-cases*. This chapter will cover the prebuilt images that offer off-the-shelf solutions based on IBM and non-IBM software products.

We will cover which product images there are readily available from the image catalog, what functionality they offer, and — not unimportantly — which licensing and pricing options there are because there are more licensing options than just bring-your-own, but more on this later. First let's look at the general differentiation of IBM and non-IBM product, in the order of which they are covered in this chapter:

- The **IBM product** images are a range of well-known IBM software products that offer enterprise-grade and often best-of-breed functionality right from the IBM® SmartCloud® Enterprise public image catalog.

  - Additionally there is a growing number of Service Instances that can be created which are bundled in IBM® SmartCloud® Application Services. Read more on IBM® SmartCloud® Application Services in *Chapter 6, Further Developments*.

- The non-IBM product images and solutions are based on **IBM Business Partners solutions**, which can be segmented into two categories:

  ○ The cloud ecosystem partner images are a diverse range of readily available images in the public image catalog. These images are all validated by IBM and can be provisioned just as easily as any other image.

  ○ The **Ready for IBM SmartCloud Services solutions** showcase features the applications, software, and tools from IBM Business Partners that run on IBM® SmartCloud®. However this does not necessarily mean that these are available as image from the image catalog or that they are suitable for IBM® SmartCloud® Enterprise at all.

Let's cover these categories one by one in the following sections.

IBM product images

Many of the IBM software products that fit the nature of cloud computing, but also applications specifically for prototyping or to support proofs of concept, are available in the public image catalog of IBM® SmartCloud® Enterprise.

Take for instance WebSphere® Application Server (WAS), which is often used as part of web-based application stack, which now can be deployed within 30 minutes to test your newly-developed J2EE application. And even better, when using the pay-as-you-go license model, you only pay for the instance and software for the time you actually have it running. This saves a lot of time to create the infrastructure, install, and configure WAS and your J2EE application. This also saves you money because you only pay for the minutes/hours/days you actually need to test your J2EE application.

At the time of writing, the list of IBM products available as public image, grouped by type of functionality offered, is:

- **Industry Application Platform:** This category is a fully configured software stack with WebSphere® Application Server, DB2® Express-C, and WebSphere MQ for developing industry applications.

- **Business Analytics:** The images in this category deliver a complete set of business analytics solutions based on Cognos® Business Intelligence as well as images for predictive models, rules, and decision logic based on SPSS®.

- **Business Process Manager:** This category contains images with business process management (BPM) platforms in several versions as well as integration and process designer software images.

- **Enterprise Content Management:** This category offers an image, based on IBM Case Manager, for uniting content, processes, and people to create a single view of a case and optimize case outcomes.

- **Information Management:** This category offers a variety of images for managing data and information. There are images available with BigInsights, Hadoop Master and Data Nodes, DB2, Informix, and InfoSphere®.

- **Collaboration:** This has ready-to-use images with collaboration suites—combining IBM Domino, Sametime, and IBM Connections—as well as several Domino and WebSphere Portal versions for useful collaboration.

- **Mobile:** For mobile there is one image at this time, based on Worklight® Server, which is designed to seamlessly integrate into the enterprise environment and leverage its existing resources and infrastructure.

- **Rational®:** This well-filled category contains nine images with Rational software and system innovation tools such as Rational Application Developer, Rational Asset Manager, Rational Build Forge, Rational Requirements Composer, Rational Software Architect, and a Rational suite for Collaborative Lifecycle Management (CLM).

- **Service management**: Essential to all IT environments are the images in this category, which delivers ready to use Tivoli® products such as Tivoli Service Automation Manager, Tivoli Live Service Manager, and Tivoli Monitoring.

- **WebSphere®:** Last but not least, WebSphere has a range of images available containing the well-known WebSphere software products such as WebSphere Application Server, WebSphere Message Broker, WebSphere Portal Server and Web Content Manager, WebSphere Service Registry, and WebSphere sMash.

Please visit `www.ibm.com/developerworks/cloud/devtest.html` for an up-to-date list of IBM products, licensing, and pricing options.

Licensing and pricing options

As you have learned in the preceding IBM product section, there are multiple licensing and pricing options for IBM products, which are same, however, for cloud ecosystem partner images. The two most used are pay-as-you-go (PAYG) and bring-your-own license (BYOL), but there are two more:

- **Bring-your-own license (BYOL)**—the most commonly available option—allows us to use previously purchased IBM software licenses.

- **Pay-as-you-go (PAYG)** model allows you to use an image with the license included. We choose the software, accept the license terms online, and receive a monthly usage bill for it.

- With the **Developer-use-only (DUO)** model we get to use software for development at no charge at all. The DUO model can be used as an eligible Independent Solution Vendor (ISV) or Systems Integrator (SI). Find more at www.ibm.com/developerworks/cloud/duo.html.

- **Pre-release** images are available on a temporary basis — for test use only — at no charge

Some images can be created using both the BYOL and PAYG license model. As a general advice for choosing the right licensing model for your specific situation, you need to evaluate the duration for which you need the image: images with a PAYG model are financially more attractive for short to midterm usage — such as proofs of concept and prototyping — whereas the BYOL models is more attractive for long-term usage scenarios — such as running production.

IBM Business Partner solutions

Next to the IBM product images available in IBM® SmartCloud® Enterprise, there is a wide variety of products available from IBM Business Partners. This significantly broadens the amount of readily available business functionality at your disposal.

To understand the vision of IBM on a cloud ecosystem, navigate to the IBM Cloud YouTube channel and watch the video *IBM Business Partners discuss the value of partnering with IBM to win in the cloud*. The YouTube channel can be found at www.youtube.com/playlist?list=PL0C1FDD0AA474D459.

As covered briefly earlier, the IBM Business Partner solutions are two-fold:

- There are the **Cloud ecosystem partner** images which are — like the IBM product images — readily available images from the IBM® SmartCloud® Enterprise public image catalog containing IBM Business Partner software products

- And there are the **Ready for IBM SmartCloud Services solutions** which are — unlike the other options — either solutions that need to be manually installed on IBM® SmartCloud® offerings — like IBM® SmartCloud® Enterprise or others — or are offered, as a service, by the IBM Business Partner and are running on an IBM® SmartCloud® offering — again, like IBM® SmartCloud® Enterprise or others.

Cloud ecosystem partner images

To start off with the IBM Business Partner solutions, we take a closer look at the list of IBM Business Partner images—bundled under the name *Cloud ecosystem partner images*. As with the IBM product images detailed earlier, these images are available off-the-shelf from the IBM® SmartCloud® Enterprise public image catalog. Let's look at this list in alphabetic order:

- **10gen (MongoDB)**: This offers you a document-oriented database, as opposed to a relational database, based on the similar named open source product.

- **Alphinat (SmartGuide)**: This gives you a development platform for cloud applications. One of the powerful features of SmartGuide is that it uses visual drag-and-drop tools to quickly build your cloud applications using web dialogs, which enhance user centricity and speed of development.

- **AppZero**: This allows you to migrate your server applications to any infrastructure cloud (IaaS), or any other traditional infrastructure for that matter. This solution enables you to move your applications with the push of a button, without re-engineering and/or re-installing it.

- **Asigra (Cloud Backup™)**: This provides you with a backup platform that enables you to protect your office and mobile IT assets such as servers, desktops, laptops, tablets, and smartphones using one intuitive solution.

- **Aviarc**: This hands you the tools to develop and deploy custom developed web-based applications from start to finish, offering a collaboration software development suite and delivery platform in one.

- **BeyondTrust (PowerBroker)**: This facilitates you in securing your data in multi-tenant environments—such as cloud computing solutions—helping you to mitigate insider threats.

- **CapCal**: This delivers to you a solution for load and/or performance testing that, using the rapid provisioning capabilities of IBM® SmartCloud® Enterprise, allows you to perform tests with nearly any number of simulated users.

- **Cohesive Flexible Technologies Corporation (VPN-Cubed™ Datacenter Connect)**: This provides you with a secure and controllable overlay network—using IPsec tunnels—without the expenses and sprawl of maintenance of traditional secure network options.

- **Convertigo**: This allows you to integrate business logic with data from many sources—such as on premise and cloud—to publish them to mobile devices or portals.

- **Corent (Multi-Tenant Server)**: This enables you to make multi-tenant SaaS solutions from virtual and single-tenant web applications.

- **Dynamic Network Services Inc. (Dyn)**: This is an infrastructure as a service (IaaS) solution that specializes in both managed DNS and e-mail delivery.

- **Kaavo**: This allows you to automate the deployment of applications in a cloud environment and manage the service levels.

- **NetEnrich (Services Gateway)**: This is a monitoring and management application that enables you to control the devices in your IT environment.

- **OpenCrowd (IdeaShare)**: This is a solution that allows you to improve your products and services by enabling you to harvest ideas, suggestions, and feedback.

- **Pragma Systems (Pragma Fortress SSH)**: This implements fast Secure Shell (SSH) server and SSH Client connectivity.

- **Protecode**: This is a hosted solution on IBM® SmartCloud® Enterprise for software product license management.

- **Radware (Alteon VA)**: This is an application delivery controller (ADC) that provides you with the tools to implement high availability, performance optimization, and complete security for IBM® SmartCloud® Enterprise and/ or on-premise applications.

- **Riverbed (Stingray Traffic Manager)**: This is a solution that can optimize and reduce your network.

- **Servoy**: This is your solution when you want to develop and deploy SaaS applications.

- **SugarCRM**: This provides an off-the-shelf customer relationship management (CRM) solution, based on the well-known open source software product.

- **TrustVault**: This implements a solution for secure e-mail messaging by triangulating a sender's identity and reputation.

- **TwinStrata™ (CloudArray™)**: This offers you advanced gateway functionality for storage services such as cloud object storage, as one of the third-party gateway options object storage.

- **Vormetric (Data Security)**: This provides you with a central console to manage your security policies and protect data inside your operating environment.

- **Zementis (ADAPA® decision engine)**: This offers a solution for predictive analytics.

Find a more elaborate description and the complete listing of cloud ecosystem partner images and their licensing options at www.ibm.com/developerworks/cloud/partner-images.html.

Ready for IBM SmartCloud Services solutions

A third ecosystem that can be utilized by IBM® SmartCloud® Enterprise users is the Ready for IBM SmartCloud Services solutions showcase which features the applications, software, and tools from IBM Business Partners that run on IBM® SmartCloud®. Note that this ecosystem has solutions for a wide variety of the IBM® SmartCloud® portfolio solutions covered in *Chapter 1, IBM® SmartCloud®*, and not for IBM® SmartCloud® Enterprise only.

In this section we will only focus on the solutions available for IBM® SmartCloud® Enterprise. All solutions in the Ready for IBM SmartCloud Services solutions showcase have gone through a validation process to ensure compatibility with one or more IBM® SmartCloud® Enterprise solutions.

The list with solutions is constantly growing as every IBM Business Partner with a valuable software solution that can demonstrate that their solution meets IBM validation criteria will be included in the ecosystem and expand the listing.

The Ready for IBM SmartCloud Services solutions are grouped in the following categories, though solutions can appear in more than one category:

- Analytics
- Business applications
- Collaboration
- Development and test
- Infrastructure services and availability
- Security, monitoring, and reporting
- Web applications

The following list covers the most relevant solutions specifically for IBM® SmartCloud® Enterprise, as this is the main subject of this book.

A big difference between the previous listing of cloud ecosystem partner images and the solutions in this list is that the latter are certified solutions but are not available as public image in the catalog: these solutions require manual installation by either you or the IBM Business Partner or the IBM Business Partner sharing the image with you.

At the time of writing the following solutions are available:

- **Assimil8 Limited (Analytics in the Cloud)**: This combines the power of cloud computing, Cognos® analytics, and additional complimentary applications in a simple way

- **Element Blue (CloudBlue Express)**: This is a consulting and services offering that enables adoption and implementation of IBM® SmartCloud® Enterprise providing turnkey implementations, training, and services support

- **Vision Solutions, Inc. (Double-Take)**: Availability combines continuous real-time replication and automatic failover capabilities for disaster recovery, high availability, and centralized back up on physical or virtual servers

- **Comptel Corporation (Comptel Social Links)**: This delivers next generation customer value management with advanced analytics powered by social intelligence

- **DFC International Ltd. (UCbyDFC)**: This integrates instant chat, presence information, telephony, video conferencing, data sharing, whiteboarding with voicemail, e-mail, SMS, and fax

- **FusionWare Integration Corp. (FusionWare dbLynx 2SQL)**: This is an easy-to-use tool for rapid migration of data from a number of relational and non-relational sources to your DB2 database

- **nViso SA (Emotion Video Analytics)**: This allows 3D facial imaging to enable marketers to identify emotions triggered by products and brand messages at a scale previously not possible

- **Class Technology Co, Ltd. (ECObjects/TotalBOM)**: This is an integrated BOM/cPDM solution that can be used throughout the product lifecycle from engineering, manufacturing, procurement, marketing, sales to after service

- **CloudPrime (Cloud-Based Application Messaging)**: This is a messaging service that enables you to build secure, easy-to-consume application interfaces and connectivity

- **Domino Soft, S.A. de C.V.**: This offers solutions based on IBM Domino such as CRM Xpress®, desk Xpress®, and doc Xpress®

- **Gigaspaces Technologies Ltd. (Cloudify)**: This offers a solution that allows on-boarding of enterprise and Big Data applications to IBM® SmartCloud® Enterprise on a massive scale without changing any code

- **Grid Robotics LLC (Cloud Lab Classroom)**: This is a virtual classroom management solution focused on ensuring that training organizations reach their eLearning business goals faster

- **JasperSoft (Business Intelligence Suite)**: This is a solution for business intelligence reporting, building on JasperReports which is a popular 100 percent Java reporting library for developers

- **Omnitrol Networks, Inc. (Retail Smart-Store Intelligence & Global Item-Level Traceability)**: This provides RFID-based item-level inventory traceability and intelligence in one solution

- **SOASTA, Inc.**: The SOASTA CloudTest® platform offers a single, integrated platform for functional and performance testing of modern web and mobile applications

- **Sonian (Archive)**: This offers a solution for e-mail archiving with features to ensure compliance and eDiscovery

- **Sproxil, Inc. Mobile Product Authentication (MPA)**: Solution leverages mobile phones and simple scratch-off labels to deliver an anti-counterfeiting solution at the consumer level

- **Trend Micro, Inc. (SecureCloud™)**: This provides data protection and control features for your confidential information by implementing an encryption service that keeps your data private and helps meet your regulatory compliance requirements

- **VACAVA Inc (Specifi)**: This is a solution for specification management, tailored for packaging, raw materials, and other finished product specifications

- **enStratus™ Networks, Inc.**: This is a cloud infrastructure management solution for deploying and managing applications in a multi-cloud architecture and delivers features such as cloud governance and automation

Find more elaborate descriptions of the Ready for IBM SmartCloud Services solutions for IBM® SmartCloud® Enterprise and an up-to-date list at `www-304.ibm.com/partnerworld/gsd/showcase.do?cd=SCS`.

Summary

In this chapter we have learned about the images in the public image catalog, both IBM and non-IBM software products, and we have covered the different licensing models for the images. We have also looked at the Ready for IBM SmartCloud Services solutions which contain solutions for running on IBM® SmartCloud® Enterprise.

In the next and final chapter, we cover the foreseeable future of IBM® SmartCloud® Enterprise and related cloud services in the IBM® SmartCloud® portfolio.

6
Further Developments

Now we have reached the final chapter of the book, let's reflect what we have learned and look forward, where possible.

We have covered the IBM® SmartCloud® portfolio from where we zoomed in on IBM® SmartCloud® Enterprise to get an in-depth view of its history, use-cases, and advanced features. We used IBM® SmartCloud® Enterprise exemplary to get a better understanding and build.

In this chapter we widen our view again, like in *Chapter 1*, *IBM® SmartCloud®*, to the platform as a service solutions on top of IBM® SmartCloud® Enterprise and take a little peek into the foreseeable future.

As mentioned in previous chapters, with IBM® SmartCloud® Enterprise, you gain access to both infrastructure services (IaaS) and platform services (PaaS), all in one cloud solution. The platform services, available through the SCE management console under **Service Instances**, are all bundled under the name of **IBM® SmartCloud® Application Services**.

Although we cannot fully predict the future, there are some valuable sources of information that I want to share with you so you can stay updated on the latest changes and announcements for future developments. Second, there are some patterns and trends that allow us to look into our crystal ball.

IBM® SmartCloud® Application Services

IBM® SmartCloud® Application Services, the platform services layer on top of IBM® SmartCloud® Enterprise, was introduced in December 2012. It delivers a collaborative, cloud-based environment that supports the full lifecycle of accelerated application development, deployment, and delivery. It provides two separate — but complementary — services: Collaborative Lifecycle Management Service and IBM® SmartCloud® Application Workload Service:

- **Collaborative Lifecycle Management Service (CLMS)** is a set of seamlessly integrated Rational® tools which provides a real-time cloud-based **collaborative environment** for accelerated application development and delivery as a platform service. It is designed to help coordinate software development activities throughout the lifecycle of an application, from requirements tracking through design, implementation, build, test, deployment, and maintenance.
- **IBM® SmartCloud® Application Workload Service (SCAWS)** allows us to use **design patterns**. A pattern consists of proven best practices and expertise for complex system tasks that have been captured, lab-tested, and optimized into a deployable form. These patterns can be very powerful because they can include policy-based automated scaling and easy duplication between IBM public and private cloud environments.

The IBM SmartCloud® Enterprise Monthly Cost Estimator, described in *Chapter 2, IBM® SmartCloud® Enterprise* supports all IBM® SmartCloud® Application Services prices and content. To learn more on its features and how get started on running your first service instances:

```
pic.dhe.ibm.com/infocenter/scasic/v1r0m0/index.jsp
```

Improving software delivery with DevOps

To support DevOps, collaborative tools are needed to support the agile service delivery approach, hence accelerating application deployment from weeks to minutes. When we combine the functionality offered by CLMS and SCAWS together, this is exactly what we get. We get one integrated DevOps solution that promotes communication, collaboration, and integration between software developers and IT operations to more rapidly produce quality software products and services.

The name DevOps is derived from a combination of the two words *dev*elopment and *op*erations. DevOps is more than a new development methodology like agile software development; it's about communication and collaboration between both the two earlier stated stakeholders and the business. It is mainly targeted at product delivery, quality testing, feature development, and maintenance releases in order to improve reliability, security, and faster development and deployment cycles.

Download this complementary e-book to gain a better understanding of DevOps and learn how it can improve the IT processes in your organization:

ow.ly/1CGGz

Valuable sources of information

IBM® SmartCloud® Enterprise and Application Services

Staying up-to-date with the latest IBM® SmartCloud® Enterprise (and Application Services) developments and announcements is vital for knowing what you can expect in the near future. The three most important sources of information are:

- The SCE management console, specifically on the **Support** page, where many resources are directly available or just one click away in the **Documentation Library**, **Video Library**, and **Asset Catalog**.

- The developerWorks® website, the IBM technical resource and professional network for the developer and IT professional, offers great in-depth articles on many of the capabilities that IBM® SmartCloud® Enterprise has, as we have seen in most prominently in *Chapter 4, Advanced Use-cases*. It can be accessed at www.ibm.com/developerworks

- The Thoughts on Cloud blog is also a great place to see what's happening and what can be done with IBM and IBM Business Partner solutions. As with the developerWorks website, the information provided here covers more about IBM® SmartCloud® Enterprise, which gives us a broader perspective on what's happening with IBM and cloud computing. It is available at thoughtsoncloud.com.

There is also **IBM SmartCloud Enterprise newsletter** containing a wealth of information on new features, use-cases, and other news. You can subscribe to these, and more, newsletters via the IBM eNewsletter Subscription Services webpage.

Then there is the **IBM SmartCloud Enterprise Developers Group**. This is a technical community composed of individuals interested in the application programming interfaces (APIs) of IBM® SmartCloud® Enterprise. The group includes IBMers and non-IBMers and covers how the APIs can be used to automate processes and build solutions that integrate with IBM® SmartCloud® Enterprise. It is available at www. ibm.com/developerworks/community/blogs/iaas_cloud.

IBM Innovation Center events

Additionally there are the IBM Innovation Center events, which offer a wide range of no-charge workshops, seminars, and briefings conducted by highly trained subject matter experts. These events help you build technical skills, learn how to market and sell more effectively with IBM, and connect with Business Partners. Some of the virtual events focus on the new possibilities of IBM® SmartCloud® solutions, and are complementary.

Global Technology Outlook

The Global Technology Outlook (GTO) is IBM Research's vision of the future for information technology (IT) and its implications on industries.

This annual exercise highlights emerging software, hardware, and services technology trends that are expected to significantly impact the IT sector in the next 3-10 years. The research document can be downloaded from www.zurich.ibm.com/pdf/isl/infoportal/Global_Technology_Outlook_2013.pdf.

IBM Academy of Technology

Lastly there is the IBM Academy of Technology (AoT) which, as the name suggests, consists of almost one thousand of IBM's technical leaders.

The academy develops a rich technical agenda each year which consists of studies, conferences, and consultancies. More importantly, the academy also produces a series of **TechNotes** which explore various areas of current and emerging technology. The TechNotes can be found at www-03.ibm.com/ibm/academy/technotes/technotes.shtml.

A glimpse into our crystal ball

When looking at the version history of IBM® SmartCloud® we can clearly see a pattern of delivering major releases twice a year, more specifically in May and December. Since the May 2013 release has just been announced and implemented—at the time of writing—it can be expected that the next major release will be announced and implemented in December 2013.

In terms of functionality, let's look at what announcements there have been on the IBM® SmartCloud® strategy and which trends there are in the marketplace.

Platform services

Platform as a service is clearly expanding the range of options you have from the cloud. We can see these IBM products and service developments; just look at the landing page of IBM for platform services—`www.ibm.com/cloud-computing/us/en/paas.html`—but also on almost all other major cloud service providers.

Specifically, we want to mention the platform services—IBM® SmartCloud® Application Services and IBM® SmartCloud® for SAP Applications—that IBM is building on top of the infrastructure services—IBM® SmartCloud® Enterprise and IBM® SmartCloud® Enterprise+. It can be expected that the range of platform services will grow over the years, expanding the possibilities that you have of getting managed and hosted middleware services right from the box (as a service).

Open cloud standards

Commitment to open standards has been a long running focus for IBM, which has become even more visible with the March 2013 announcement that IBM cloud software and services will be based on open standards. This move will ensure that innovation in cloud computing is not hampered by locking businesses into proprietary islands of insecure and difficult-to-manage offerings.

As the first step, IBM will base a new private cloud solution—part of the IBM® SmartCloud® Foundation portfolio segment—on the open sourced OpenStack® software. This will allow organizations to build a private cloud without the fear of being locked in, as well as allowing easier integration with public cloud solutions. It can be expected that this will surely resonate in further IBM® SmartCloud® Enterprise developments as well.

Apart from the infrastructure focused OpenStack standard, IBM is also working on platform focused standards such as OASIS® TOSCA and data interface standards such as W3C Linked Data. Not to forget the standardization bodies such as The Open Group® and user groups such as Cloud Standards Customer Council (CSCC) and Cloud Computing Use Case Discussion Group.

Find an overview of the all open cloud standards and links to each open standard individually can be found at www.ibm.com/cloud-computing/us/en/open-standards.html and a more in-depth view on the more technical open standards at www.ibm.com/developerworks/cloud/library/cl-open-architecture.

SoftLayer Technologies Inc.

On July 8th, IBM announced that it completed the acquisition of Softlayer Technologies Inc. (Softlayer), which joins IBM's new cloud services division and will be combined with IBM® SmartCloud® into a global platform. As quoted from the press release, found at www-03.ibm.com/press/us/en/pressrelease/41430.wss you can read the potency of the acquisition:

> *"SoftLayer will enable IBM to deliver an industry first: marrying the security, privacy and reliability of private clouds with the economy and speed of a public cloud. SoftLayer offers a breakthrough capability that provides a cloud "on ramp" for born-on-the-web companies, government, and the Fortune 500."*

An interesting, analyst, view on the Softlayer acquisition and the growth potential for the IBM® SmartCloud® portfolio can be viewed in the video at www.youtube.com/watch?v=a3uscmcQVTI

Hybrid cloud

Hybrid cloud, combining both public and private cloud services into a solution, looks like the most powerful delivery form for the years to come. Powerful in the sense that you get to choose from the mix of characteristics that both private and public cloud solutions offer. To underline the trend, many analysts believe that 2013 will be the year that hybrid cloud implementations will truly get traction.

With IBM's broad and integrated family of cloud technologies, the IBM® SmartCloud® portfolio covered in *Chapter 1, IBM® SmartCloud®*, IBM is perfectly placed to deliver hybrid cloud solutions. IBM, for instance, has solutions for integrating multi-source, multi-vendor cloud solutions, allowing application portability and central system and server management.

Another example of application portability in a hybrid cloud is the use of design patterns—allowing you to define your infrastructure topology, including application code and scalability characteristics into a reusable asset—in both IBM's public and private cloud solutions. The developerWorks article series *Inside the hybrid cloud* takes you through all aspects of the value and impact of implementing and using a hybrid cloud.

1. The first article, *Redefine services and delivery methods*, covers the basics of a hybrid cloud implementation, takes you through the services it makes available, and provides a point of view on the potential business value. The article is available at www.ibm.com/developerworks/cloud/library/cl-hybridcloud1.

2. *Federation is key to XaaS*, the second article, describes hybrid cloud in more detail and focuses on the principle of a federated cloud: orchestrating multiple cloud solutions as if it were one solution. It is available at www.ibm.com/developerworks/cloud/library/cl-hybridcloud2.

3. The article *Administration* peeks under the hood of hybrid cloud to see what it takes to make the hybrid powerhouse a reality. It can be viewed at www.ibm.com/developerworks/cloud/library/cl-hybridcloud3

4. *Implementation considerations*, the final article of the series, looks into the aspect of implementing and consuming a hybrid cloud setup like governance, network connectivity, and access control. This article is available at www.ibm.com/developerworks/cloud/library/cl-hybridcloud4

Summary

With this chapter we have reached the end of this book; closing the loop from the IBM cloud strategy and IBM® SmartCloud® portfolio, through fine-grained information on IBM® SmartCloud® Enterprise, and reaching towards a high-level view where IBM® SmartCloud® might be heading in the near future.

A Brief History

When IBM® SmartCloud® Enterprise was launched back in 2010, it was originally known as IBM Smart Business Development and Test on the IBM Cloud. The reason for this was that the market, at that time, was looking for solutions supporting development and test workloads. Once the market changed towards a demand for production workloads, the naming of the solution was changed to the current one.

In the following figure the history of IBM® SmartCloud® Enterprise is shown, depicting the timing and most important features of each release.

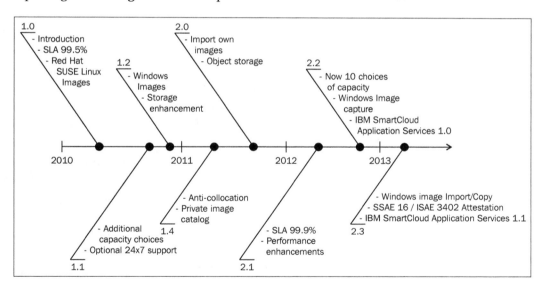

Further elaborating on this figure; the remainder of this appendix covers these major releases of IBM® SmartCloud® Enterprise (with availability date) in chronological order and elaborates on the main improvements relative to the previous version.

Note the introduction of IBM® SmartCloud® Application Services (release 1.0) in the release of Version 2.2 of IBM® SmartCloud® Enterprise, which shows the tight integration and stacking of these public cloud services.

- **Release 1.0** (May 2010) has the following features:
    - ° Self-provisioning of images consisting of base images with either Red Hat Linux® or SUSE Linux operating systems
    - ° Additional IBM software images that can be configured as per your selection
    - ° Access to and use of software images in the catalog, charged either on an hourly rate basis or using current valid license entitlements obtained under a separate IBM agreement
    - ° Raw compute power with virtual machines, persistent storage, and static IP addresses
    - ° Monthly usage-based billing that supports enterprise purchase order procurement and invoices
    - ° Support consisting of self-service access to documentation and forums
    - ° Service level agreements based on service availability of 99.5% and 24 x 7 monitoring and management of the managing infrastructure

- **Release 1.1** (August 2010) has the following features:
    - ° Virtual machine instances from a selection of seven standard machine configurations consisting of CPU capacity, virtual memory, and storage
    - ° Additional persistent storage and static IP addresses provisioned on demand and VPN/VLAN network segmentation
    - ° Additional IBM software images loaded from a catalog during the provisioning process
    - ° Optional 24 x 7 premium-level telephone support

- **Release 1.2** (November 2010) has the following features:
    - ° Enabled to provision Microsoft® Windows® operating images
    - ° Enhanced cross-enterprise collaboration through communities to share images
    - ° Capability to mount multiple persistent blocks of disk to an instance

- **Release 1.4** (March 2011) has the following features:
    - 24 x 7 premium support with service level agreements and support for Group 1 Languages (English, French, Italian, Spanish, German, Portuguese, Japanese, Chinese-Mandarin, and Korean)
    - Anti-collocation support for instances, available through application programming interfaces (APIs) only, providing the ability to provision instances on separate nodes
    - Software bundles for private images allowing users to attach a bundle, with additional configuration or software installation, to a private image and save that image after the bundle has been attached

- **Release 2.0** (December 2011) has the following features:
    - Ability to provision instances with your own operating system and license
    - Ability to use third-party tools to custom-build software images, allowing users to import their own virtual machine images into the IBM Cloud or create an image from a public or private image catalog
    - Ability to move and copy images, allowing users to transfer images across IBM® SmartCloud® Enterprise cloud data centers
    - Ability to mount multiple persistent blocks of disk to an instance and enhanced storage location flexibility for users through self-service tools and capacity up to 10 TB
    - Utilization and billing enhancements for customer internal use charge back and feature enhancements to help reduce customer account management time
    - IBM® SmartCloud® Enterprise object storage capability via Nirvanix, Inc., a third-party storage solution provider, providing clients with a solution designed to support millions of users, billions of objects, and Exabytes of data

- **Release 2.1** (May 2012) has the following features:
    - New service level agreement (SLA) of 99.9% SmartCloud Enterprise gives clients confidence in factoring cloud-centric applications for a broad array of workloads
    - Two new Red Hat Enterprise Linux operating systems; Version 5.8 and Version 6.2

- Upgrades to the persistent storage system, enabling increased speed and performance, and upgrades to embedded kernel-based virtual machine (KVM) hypervisors providing greater security and performance improvements

- **Release 2.2** (December 2012) has the following features:
  - Microsoft™ Windows™ Instance Capture — ability to create a true clone of an instance without the use of the Sysprep process
  - Windows Import Copy (initial release / limited availability) — ability to import a Microsoft image built outside of the IBM® SmartCloud®
  - Windows 2012 (initial release / limited availability) — support for Microsoft Windows Server 2012
  - APIs for guest messaging — provides a capability for customers to monitor the health of their SmartCloud Enterprise instances by issuing guest messages
  - Platinum M2 — provides a new virtual machine with 16vCPU, 32 GB memory, and 2 TB storage to customers to meet their memory-intensive workloads
  - IBM® SmartCloud® Application Services release 1.0

- **Release 2.3** (May 2013) has the following features:
  - Windows™ Import/Copy allows users to import Windows Server virtual images from an existing environment into IBM® SmartCloud® Enterprise as well as transfer images between data centers
  - Announcing the availability of a year-round trial of both our infrastructure and platform as a service offerings, IBM® SmartCloud® Enterprise and IBM® SmartCloud® Application Services
  - SSAE 16 / ISAE 3402 Attestation, announcing the availability of the SOC 1 report (SSAE 16 / ISAE 3402) for the IBM® SmartCloud® Enterprise offering
  - IBM® SmartCloud® Application Services release 1.1

 Find all the details of the latest version on the **Support** page of the IBM® SmartCloud® Enterprise self-service web portal in the document *What's new in IBM SmartCloud Enterprise*.

Index

J

Java API 52
Java REST API Client 53

K

Kernel-based Virtual Machine (KVM) 66

L

Linux, Apache, MySQL, PHP (LAMP) 38

M

maintenance windows 24
Mandatory Access Control (MAC) 66
measured service 8
mobile device
  virtual machine instance, monitoring from
    69
Monthly Cost Estimator
  about 22, 27, 28
  URL 28

N

network access methods 23
network concepts 66
network options
  about 25, 26
  reserved IP addresses 26
  VLAN 26
  VPN 26
network security 65
network tools 66

O

on-demand self-service 8
open cloud standards
  about 85
  URL 86

P

PaaS
  about 9, 85
  URL 85

Pay-as-you-go (PAYG) 73
persistent storage. *See* block storage
platform as a service. *See* PaaS
premium services, IBM® SmartCloud®
    Enterprise
  about 25
  network options 25, 26
  ordering 30
  storage options 25
  support options 25, 27
premium support
  advantages 27
private deployment model 10
private image catalog 23
proxy
  used, for integrating authentication policy
    66
public deployment model 10
public image catalog 23

R

Rapid Deployment Service. *See* RDS
rapid elasticity 8
Rational® 73
RDS
  about 45
  using 46
Ready for IBM SmartCloud Services
    solutions
  about 72, 74, 77-79
  category 77
  list 78, 79
Remote Desktop Protocol (RDP) 44
Representational State Transfer API. *See*
    REST API
reserved IP addresses 26
resource, IBM® SmartCloud® Enterprise
  Address 36
  attributes 36-38
  Image 36
  Instance 36
  InstanceType 36
  Key 37
  Location 36
  relationships 36-38
  SoftwareBundle 37

VLAN 36
Volume 37
VPN 36
resource pooling 8
REST API
about 52
used, for creating virtual machine instance
55, 57
used, for provisioning virtual machine
instance 53
using, from browser 54
RESTClient
installing 55

S

SaaS 9
SCAWS 82
Secure Shield Internet connectivity
features 65
Service Level Agreement (SLA) 27
Service Management 73
service models, cloud computing
about 9
BPaaS 9
IaaS 9
PaaS 9
SaaS 9
service oriented architecture (SOA) 6
shared image catalog 23
Simple Product Installation (SPiN) 46
SmartCloud Application Services. *See* **IBM**
SCAS
SmartCloud Application Workload Service.
See **SCAWS**
software as a service. *See* **SaaS**
software delivery
improving, with DevOps 82
SSH key
creating 40
storage capabilities
used, for backup 68
storage options
about 25
block storage 25
support options
about 25, 27

add-on operating system support 27
advanced premium support 27
premium support 27

T

TechNotes
URL 84

U

User Agent Switcher 54
user guide, API 53
users guide 47

V

virtual local area network. *See* **VLAN**
virtual local storage 23
virtual machine instance
about 22
block storage volume, creating 40
configuring 44
connecting to 43
consuming 44
creating 41-43
creating, REST API used 55, 57
image, customizing 46
monitoring 69
monitoring, from mobile device 69
monitoring, IBM Tivoli® Monitoring used
69
provisioning 38, 39
provisioning, REST API used 53
RDS, using 46
snapshot, creating 44
snapshot, taking 45
SSH key, creating 40
virtual private network. *See* **VPN**
VLAN 23, 26
VPN 23, 26

W

WebSphere® 73
Windows Import/Copy default feature 63

Thank you for buying
IBM® SmartCloud® Essentials

About Packt Publishing

Packt, pronounced 'packed', published its first book "Mastering phpMyAdmin for Effective MySQL Management" in April 2004 and subsequently continued to specialize in publishing highly focused books on specific technologies and solutions.

Our books and publications share the experiences of your fellow IT professionals in adapting and customizing today's systems, applications, and frameworks. Our solution based books give you the knowledge and power to customize the software and technologies you're using to get the job done. Packt books are more specific and less general than the IT books you have seen in the past. Our unique business model allows us to bring you more focused information, giving you more of what you need to know, and less of what you don't.

Packt is a modern, yet unique publishing company, which focuses on producing quality, cutting-edge books for communities of developers, administrators, and newbies alike. For more information, please visit our website: www.packtpub.com.

About Packt Enterprise

In 2010, Packt launched two new brands, Packt Enterprise and Packt Open Source, in order to continue its focus on specialization. This book is part of the Packt Enterprise brand, home to books published on enterprise software – software created by major vendors, including (but not limited to) IBM, Microsoft and Oracle, often for use in other corporations. Its titles will offer information relevant to a range of users of this software, including administrators, developers, architects, and end users.

Writing for Packt

We welcome all inquiries from people who are interested in authoring. Book proposals should be sent to author@packtpub.com. If your book idea is still at an early stage and you would like to discuss it first before writing a formal book proposal, contact us; one of our commissioning editors will get in touch with you.

We're not just looking for published authors; if you have strong technical skills but no writing experience, our experienced editors can help you develop a writing career, or simply get some additional reward for your expertise.

Amazon Web Services: Migrating your .NET Enterprise Application

ISBN: 978-1-84968-194-0   Paperback: 336 pages

Evaluate your Cloud requirements and successfully migrate your .NET Enterprise application to the Amazon Web Services Platform

1. Get to grips with Amazon Web Services from a Microsoft Enterprise .NET viewpoint

2. Fully understand all of the AWS products including EC2, EBS, and S3

3. Quickly set up your account and manage application security

4. Learn through an easy-to-follow sample application with step-by-step instructions

OpenNebula 3 Cloud Computing

ISBN: 978-1-84951-746-1   Paperback: 314 pages

Set-up, manage, and maintain your Cloud and learn solutions for datacenter virtualization with this step-by-step practical guide

1. Take advantage of open source distributed file-systems for storage scalability and high-availability

2. Build-up, manage and maintain your Cloud without previous knowledge of virtualization and cloud computing

3. Install and configure every supported hypervisor: KVM, Xen, VMware

Please check **www.PacktPub.com** for information on our titles

Oracle Enterprise Manager Cloud Control 12c: Managing Data Center Chaos

Oracle Enterprise Manager Cloud Control 12c: Managing Data Center Chaos

Get to grips with the latest innovative techniques for managing data center chaos including performance tuning, security compliance, patching and more.

Porus Homi Havewala
Oracle Certified Master

Oracle Enterprise Manager Cloud Control 12c: Managing Data Center Chaos

ISBN: 978-1-84968-478-1   Paperback: 394 pages

Get to grips with the latest innovative techniques for managing data center chaos including performance tuning, security compliance, patching and more.

1. Learn about the tremendous capabilities of the latest powerhouse version of Oracle Enterprise Manager 12c Cloud Control

2. Take a deep dive into crucial topics including Provisioning and Patch Automation, Performance Management and Exadata Database Machine Management

3. Take advantage of the author's experience as an Oracle Certified Master in this real world guide including enterprise examples and case studies

OpenStack Cloud Computing Cookbook

Over 100 recipes to successfully set up and manage your OpenStack cloud environments with complete coverage of Nova, Swift, Keystone, Glance, and Horizon.

Kevin Jackson

OpenStack Cloud Computing Cookbook

ISBN: 978-1-84951-732-4   Paperback: 318 pages

Over 100 recipes to successfully set up and manage your OpenStack cloud environments with complete coverage of Nova, Swift, Keystone, Glance, and Horizon.

1. Develop your Java applications using JDBC and Oracle JDeveloper

2. Explore the new features of JDBC 4.0

3. Use JDBC and the data tools in Oracle JDeveloper

Please check **www.PacktPub.com** for information on our titles

www.ingramcontent.com/pod-product-compliance
Lightning Source LLC
Chambersburg PA
CBHW060159060326
40690CB00018B/4169